Strategy, Planning & Litigating To Win

Orchestrating Trial Outcomes with Systems
Theory, Psychology, Military Science, and
Utility Theory

A. S. Dreier

First Published in 2012 by CONATUS PRESS

© 2012 A. S. Dreier

ISBN: 0615676952
ISBN-13: 978-0615676951

CONTENTS

1 ➤ THE NEED FOR FORMAL STRATEGY

Chance favors the prepared mind.[1]

Tactics without strategy is the noise before defeat.[2]

The reach and effectiveness of litigation strategy can be vastly enhanced and training in litigation strategy could be greatly improved by augmenting current trial advocacy methods with a strategic framework that integrates proven concepts and techniques of military science, utility theory, psychology, and systems theory.

Trial advocacy offers an array of well-developed tactics (i.e., methods for voir dire, opening statement, direct- and cross-examination, admitting evidence, and so on).[3] Tactics, however, are immediate actions for

---

[1] Eric D. Beinhocker, *Creating Strategy in an Unknowable Universe*, Jun. 19, 2006, Harvard Business School Working Knowledge Archive (Dec. 2, 2011, 10:23AM), http://hbswk.hbs.edu/archive/5387.html#37 (quoting Louis Pasteur).

[2] Gian P. Gentile, *Counterinsurgency and War, in* THE OXFORD HANDBOOK OF WAR 398 (Julian Lindley French, Yves Boyer eds. 2012) (quoting Sun Tzu)[though often used, I cannot find this quote in this form in either the Griffith or the Sawyer translations of THE ART OF WAR]

[3] *See generally* THOMAS A MAUET TRIAL TECHNIQUES 250 (6th ed. 2002) (Consider the limited goals of the referenced actions. For example, *voir dire*: "your specific purposes [are to] . . . Present yourself and your party in a favorable light . . . [l]earn about the jurors beliefs and attitudes . . . [and f]amiliarize the jurors with applicable legal and factual concepts." Regarding cross examination: "There are two basic

immediate needs.[4]   Strategy looks not to immediate needs but to overarching goals.[5]   Where a tactic can be used to discredit a witness, strategy would merge that witness's testimony into the broader scheme of achieving the final verdict or even some goal beyond the verdict. While tactics move one from B to C, strategy coordinates the entire interaction from A to Z. Strategy can anticipate events, integrate tactical actions, and shape the emerging situation with coherent focus.[6]

For strategy, trial advocacy literature offers the constructs of theme and theory, and the advice to write one's closing argument first to clarify what their case must establish.[7] While noting the need to integrate motions, evidence presentation, and other tactical actions around the theme and

---

purposes . . . [e]liciting favorable testimony . . . [and] asking the kinds of questions that will discredit the witness or his testimony."). These are immediate actions for immediate needs. *See also* STEVEN LUBET, NITA MODERN TRIAL ADVOCACY: ANALYSIS AND PRACTICE 422-25 (2004).

[4] U.S. MARINE CORPS, MARINE CORPS DOCTRINAL PUB. (MCDP) 1-3, TACTICS 3 (1997).

[5] *Cf.* U.S. MARINE CORPS, MARINE CORPS DOCTRINAL PUB. (MCDP) 1-1, STRATEGY 37 (1997) ("Strategy, broadly defined, is the process of interrelating ends and means. . . Our primary interest is . . . to secure the objectives of national policy.").

[6] *See, e.g.,* CELINE FRANCIS, CONFLICT RESOLUTION AND STATUS 34 (2011) ("[S]trategy integrates the sequence of actions, namely the programme that is needed to attain the major objective.").

[7] *See, e.g.,* LUBET, *supra* note 3, at 8-10; DENT GITCHEL & MOLLY TOWNES O'BRIEN, TRIAL ADVOCACY BASICS 16-25, 240 (2006). Writing the closing first suggests the attorney should answer the strategic questions of, "Where do I want to go?" and "How am I going to get there?" *See, e.g.,* THOMAS A. MAUET, MAUET'S TRIAL NOTEBOOK 15 (2nd ed. 1998) ("[P]lanning the closing argument first will tell you what to emphasize and what to cover lightly, or not at all, in the other stages of trial."). This, unfortunately leaves the attorney to fabricate the answers to "where" and "how" in an unstructured, *ad hoc* fashion (a situation this article seeks to rectify). Note, however, that strategy as detailed within does not limit the goal to one within the merits of the case. Rather it can reach to sentencing, and even to cases wholly outside the immediate litigation.

theory, textbooks offers few if any specific methods, or even general principles, for completing this integration.[8]

While absent from the literature, methods for anticipating events, integrating tactics, and (to an extent) shaping situations abound in practice (nearly every attorney puts thought into how to best assemble his case). These methods are empirical, however, unwritten and in most cases driven by the attorney's *feel* for the situation and *notions* of how a given jury or witness will respond.[9]   Whether highly effective or otherwise, these individual, intuitive[10] methods offer no common vocabulary or studied best practices, and no defined understanding of their limitations.[11]   The failure

---

[8]   *See, e.g.*, LUBET *supra* note 3. The text refers to strategy most often as simply a preplanned tactic. "[T]here is no reason to postpone the objection decision until the very moment when the answer is falling from the witnesses lips. . . . Objection *strategy* should therefore be planned in the same manner as is direct or cross examination." *Id.* at 269 (emphasis added). "A further *strategy* [as opposed to an *element* of your overarching strategy] is to utilize voir dire as a means of testing jurors' reactions to aspects of the case." *Id.* at 546 (emphasis added). Witness impeachment is a strategy. *Id.* at 206. Producing exhibits is a strategy. *Id.* at 382. Explaining away an inconsistency is a strategy. *Id.* at 504. Lubet does, however, use strategy in the context of integrating elements of the larger case with regard to considerations in calling a hostile witness. *Id.* at 77-78. *See also* Colonel Melinda L. Davis-Perritano, *An Application of Clausewitzian Military Strategic Thought to Trial Practice*, 37(2), THE REPORTER 12 (Summer 2010) ("It is important for trial counsel to truly appreciate that case theory and strategy are two separate but related functions.").

[9]   Richard K. Neumann Jr., *On Strategy*, 59 FORDHAM L. REV. 319-25 (1990) ("[b]ecause lawyers and other professionals have not been able to codify the processes through which they arrive at solutions such as diagnoses and strategies, inquiry into those processes is muted, and the sources of professional superiority are obscured behind labels like "wisdom," "talent" and intuition.") (citing D. SCHON, EDUCATING THE REFLECTIVE PRACTITIONER 12-13 (1985)). *See also* Davis-Perritano *supra* note 8, at 11-18 ("It is a daunting task to develop a litigation strategy . . . The challenge is in developing the judgment necessary.").

[10]   "[I]ntuitive judgments are hypotheses based on personal convictions, supporting evidence is hidden and vague." TONY BASTICK, INTUITION: HOW WE THINK AND ACT 26 (1982) (citing MORRIS L. BIGGE & MAURICE P. HUNT, PSYCHOLOGICAL FOUNDATIONS OF EDUCATION (1965)).

[11]   *See, e.g.*, Lynn M. LoPucki & Walter O. Weyrauch, *A Theory of Legal Strategy*, 49 DUKE L.J. 1405, 1410 (2000) ("Legal strategy is curiously absent from the realm of legal theory"); Neumann, *supra* note 9, at 300 ("[S]trategic creativity in law has not been rigorously studied.").

to capture these techniques in concrete form and to understand their full capabilities and limitations reduces the individual attorney's effectiveness, and creates deficiencies in the training of apprentice trial advocates.[12]

This article offers a system for building litigation strategy, one of many possible approaches, but one entirely based upon *studied* strategic principles with an established vocabulary and *concrete, proven* methods. This framework accommodates existing techniques of game theory and military and business strategy, readily allowing attorneys to incorporate their further knowledge of these areas into the methodology. It is scalable and modular, adapting to whatever time and effort the attorney can devote to strategy. The attorney can adopt it in whole or in part, producing thorough, hard copy strategies, or working through the constructs mentally, focusing only on specific areas of the coming trial that deserve the most attention. And, the fact that the discipline of Strategy[13] has a developed vocabulary means it can be communicated in training attorneys and law students in trial advocacy.

The framework herein offers both a way of thinking about strategy and a specific method of producing it—a product and a process. As an integrated philosophy and method, this framework endeavors to ensure:

1. The attorney's plan is valid:
   o comprehensively addressing the situation, and
   o standing a reasonable probability of success.

2. All actions are:
   o focused,
   o integrated and mutually supportive, and
   o appropriately sequenced to achieve the purpose.

3. The attorney is capable of:
   o rapidly adapting to changing situations,
   o increasing the number of potential opportunities,
   o shaping the situation and the opponent's actions,
   o responding with a scalable modular system applicable to trials of any complexity level, and

---

[12] Neumann, *supra* note 9, at 319-25.

[13] Or perhaps "disciplines" if the reader considers military science and business strategy to be distinct—a view I hope will be reconsidered after reading this book.

     o   ultimately achieving the strategic purpose in a changing, uncertain environment.

    The core of this framework draws upon military science, merging the military theory of maneuver with the Counterinsurgency[14]-style Line of Operations. Maneuver theory is based on the Observe-Orient-Decide-Act (OODA) Loop (depicted in Figure 1), a construct that emphasizes swift, intelligent action (moving through to the final "Act" phase of the Loop as rapidly and as often as possible) as the key to success in conflict.

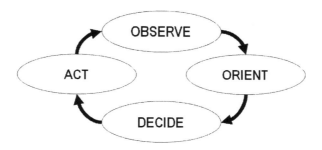

Figure 1: The OODA Loop[15]

    This book will demonstrate how maneuver philosophy is as applicable to litigation as it is to war and business,[16] and how attorneys can use it to

---

[14] U. S. Dep't of Army, Field Manual (FM) 3-24, Counterinsurgency 5-3 – 5-17 (2006) [hereinafter FM 3-24]. Note that while the FM uses the acronym "LLO" to denote that these are Logical Lines of Operation (as opposed to map-based, geographic Lines of Operation), in practice (perhaps because of the non-linear nature of our current conflicts) LLOs are not verbally differentiated from other Lines of Operation. Because the phrase "Line of Operation" holds in practice, that term is used in this article. The acronym "LOO" for (Line of Operations) is not used in order to minimize the confusion between OODA Loops and LOOs that occurred when that acronym was relied upon in the training product and earlier drafts of this article.

[15] Frans P. B. Osinga, Science, Strategy and War: The Strategic Theory of John Boyd 2 (2007) This is the common, simplified depiction of John Boyd's OODA Loop (which will serve our needs here). The expanded version, the only version Boyd personally diagramed, appears in Osinga. *Id.* at 231.

[16] On the OODA Loop's applicability to business, see generally Chet Richards, *Certain to Win* (2004). It was originally designed for combat. *See, e.g.,* Osinga, *supra* note 155, at 4.

produce overwhelming successes in trial after trial. In accordance with maneuver theory, an attorney will adapt to developing situations rapidly and decisively (i.e., by tightening his own OODA Loop) while understanding and being able to defend against actions intended to disrupt, expand, overload his Loop, or to otherwise shape his actions. Figure 2 summarizes the methods for affecting OODA Loops that this article will discuss.

Tighten/Speed

❑**Planning the Line of Operations**
  • Rational Predictions
  • Validated Actions
  • Identified Contingencies

❑**Adapting the Line of Operations**
  • Situational Awareness
  • Flexible Plan
  • Clear Purpose & Main Effort

Understand & Defend Against

❑**Disruption & Task Overload**

❑**Expansion, Ambiguity & Deception**

❑**Decisions & Actions being shaped**

Figure 2: Methods of Affecting OODA Loops

This framework counters the premise that tactical prowess—the ability to deliver argument, cross-examine hostile witnesses, and so on—is the most beneficial skill set a trial attorney can pursue.[17] Tactical skill, we shall see, remains a requirement. So, to be clear, this framework attempts to enhance without in any way supplanting current notions of trial advocacy. By integrating tactics into a cohesive, internally-consistent plan of focused, mutually-supportive actions, however, strategy allows attorneys to achieve greater impact with those tactics, and with the evidence and argument available.[18] Attorneys are able to make more impactful, more focused

---

[17] *Cf.* SUN TZU, ART OF WAR 111 (Roger T. Ames trans. 1993) ("[T]o win a hundred victories in a hundred battles is not the highest excellence; the highest excellence is to subdue the enemy's army without fighting at all."). "Battles," of course, should be understood as individual exchanges with opposing counsel and witnesses. Also, to emphasize a point that will be clarified *infra*, subduing the enemy is never the goal—the strategically-minded attorney will focus on achieving his purpose, not on fighting his opponent.

[18] *Cf.* U. S. DEP'T OF ARMY, FIELD MANUAL (FM) 3-90, TACTICS 8-16 (2001) [hereinafter FM 3-90] (mutual support increases the strength of all positions).

decisions with greater speed in the midst of the trial.[19] Moreover, litigators can even broaden their span of effect, shaping situations beyond the immediate litigation, such as the relationships between parties, and events within other cases.[20] Maneuver philosophy in particular (the frame within which strategy is presented here) offers attorneys an option to leverage their intelligence, creativity, and determination to vastly improve their chances against better-resourced opponents with stronger cases.[21]

A. Efficacy

In my first year as a trial advocate, I tried five contested[22] cases, losing two (40%) of them. I spent the next nine months at the Marine Corps Amphibious Warfare School (AWS) studying military methods generally and maneuver warfare in particular, and then tried another twenty-eight contested cases, incorporating the strategic concepts I had learned at AWS. I was successful in all but one (3.5% loss rate). By incorporating maneuver and related strategic concepts, I improved my success rate at trial to 96.5% while trying cases of increasing complexity and facing a broader array of counsel with a higher average level of experience.

The framework presented below clarifies and expounds upon the foundational concepts taught at AWS, retroactively identifying and clarifying the specific, well-developed strategic principles underlying my

---

[19] *See* WAYNE WEITEN, PSYCHOLOGY: THEMES & VARIATIONS 249-50 (7th ed. 2008) ("quick, one-reason decision-making strategies [have demonstrated] that they can yield inferences that are just as accurate as much more elaborate and time-consuming strategies that carefully weigh many factors").

[20] Examples of "shaping relationships" and "creating effects within other cases" are discussed in relation to the case study *infra* Chapter 5, part C., where the prosecutor is trying to reduce the percentage of cases the defense bar is contesting against his overburdened office, and to convince a recalcitrant accused to testify against an alleged co-conspirator.

[21] *C.f.* WILLIAM LIND, MANEUVER WARFARE HANDBOOK 2 (1985) ("Maneuver . . . is a way of fighting smart, of out-thinking an opponent you may not be able to overpower with brute strength.").

[22] Contested here means that there was some form of legal maneuvering other than negotiation of a plea agreement or dismissal due to non-litigation developments. Success means conviction if in the role of prosecutor and dismissal of all charges (as the result of litigation) or full acquittal if in the role of defense counsel.

improvement. The core principles herein are catalogued within systems theory, psychology, and utility theory—disciplines within which they were validated through analysis and peer-reviewed scientific studies or discourse.[23] The techniques have been field tested in corporate action, diplomacy, and war—relied upon when vast sums of money and thousands of lives hung in the balance.[24] All of this offers both theoretical and practical validation of this framework.

---

[23] For Systems Theory, and its related fields of Complexity and Chaos Theory (all referenced in preparing the system herein), helpful works citing the original studies include Donella H. Meadow's *Thinking in Systems* (2008), and M. Mitchell Waldrop's *Complexity, the Emerging Science at the Edge of Order and Chaos* (1993) (an intellectual history of the development of Complexity Theory). In the field of psychology a broad sampling of subspecialties prevents a succinct list here, however a foundation relevant to the material herein can be found in Daniel Kahneman, Paul Slovic, and Amos Tversky's *Judgment Under Uncertainty: Heuristics and Biases* (1982). A mass of studies in Utility Theory are referenced in Salvador Barbera, Peter Hammond, and Christian Seidl's two volume *Handbook of Utility Theory* (2004). Utility Theory's subordinate science of Game Theory is explained (with references cited) in Avinash K.Dixit and Barry J. Nalebuff's *The Art of Strategy* (2010) and Adam M. Brandenburger and Barry J. Nalebuff's *Coopetition* (1998).

[24] Regarding the use of the OODA Loop in modern warfare, see, e.g., Robert Coram, *Boyd* 424 (2002) (quoting then-U.S. Secretary of Defense Richard Cheney stating with regard to Operation Desert Storm that when instructing General Norman Schwartkopf to revise his very direct, attrition-based original plan, "[Boyd] clearly was a factor in my thinking."). Regarding the use of Maneuver in the more recent war in Iraq, see, e.g., Colonel Nicholas E. Reynolds' *Basrah, Baghdad, and Beyond* 15-45 (2005); Jack Kelly's *Little-Known Pilot Shaped U.S. Strategy in Iraq* in the *Post-Gazette*, Mar. 21, 2003, (at http://www.post-gazette.com/nation/20030321boydnatp5.asp). Bridging the line between government and industry, see R. Preston McAfee & John McMillan, *Analyzing the Airwaves Auction*, 10(1) *J. of Econ. Perspectives* 159-75 (Winter 1996) (The FCC used game theory to design the auction of cellular band width to raise billions of dollars. The article quotes *Forbes* magazine (July 3, 1995) as stating, "Game theory, long an intellectual pastime came into its own as a business tool"). The maximization of utility is central to business. *See, e.g.,* PATRICK PRIMEAUX & JOHN STEIBER, PROFIT MAXIMIZATION: THE ETHICAL MANDATE OF BUSINESS (1995). Also, of course, Sun Tzu's, *Art of War* gained widespread notoriety for its use as a business strategy guide following its appearance in the film *Wall Street* (20th Century Fox 1987). This is, of course in addition to the reliance upon Sun Tzu's methods made by Mao Tse-tung, General Giap of Vietnam, and Admiral Yamamoto of World War II, among other military figures of noted effectiveness. RALPH D. SAWYER, THE TAO OF SPYCRAFT 620 (2004).

To assess the effectiveness of the interdisciplinary concepts herein inside the courtroom two further steps were taken. First, focus groups of trial attorneys ranging in experience from recent law school graduates to litigators of twenty or more contested trials underwent training on an abridged, rough-cut (comparatively primitive) version of the framework herein, then completed surveys and offered commentary.[25] Second, the concepts discussed were used to prepare a University of Virginia (UVA) School of Law Mock Trial Team for a short-notice competition.[26] These two evaluations transformed the nascent system into the fully developed and integrated framework presented herein, and offer some insight into its effectiveness.

The focus groups took part in live presentations (the participants in these groups were all volunteers, and so pre-disposed to be open to the subject matter), or viewed a recording of the presentation on-line[27] (this group included professionally-obligated non-volunteers—i.e., individuals with no identifiable predispositions). The results of both sets of surveys appear as Appendix A to this book.

Of the group containing non-volunteers, seventy-five percent felt that training in the preliminary version of the framework noticeably improved their understanding of the competitive interaction at trial.[28] Seventy percent felt it would additionally be useful outside of trial practice.[29] Eighty percent felt the offensive (attack-oriented) material would improve their practice,[30] and eighty-five percent felt the defensive material would improve their

---

[25] Volunteers attended live presentations, and a mix of volunteers and professionally obligated non-volunteers viewed a lecture via on-line streaming media. Participants were asked to complete and anonymously submit a survey.

[26] Peter James Johnson '49 Civil Rights Trial Competition, St. John's University School of Law (Oct. 20-21, 2011).

[27] TRIAL SHOCK & AWE, http://160.138.10.141/MediaSiteEX5_0/Viewer/?peid=c48875c3ae044355805ae3 50e86fbeb51d .

[28] *See infra* Appendix A, part II. On-Line Presentation Survey Data, question 6, item 1.

[29] *See id.* item 2.

[30] *See id.* item 5 (minimizing one's own friction).

practice.[31]   At least ninety-five percent intend to use at least some portion of the material presented in their future trial practice.[32]   These results are depicted in Figure 3.

Figure 3: Selection of On-Line Focus Group Survey Results

Two of the comments from focus group members were noteworthy. First, one attorney offered that he had inadvertently used one of the techniques described in the training and it had proven successful.[33]   This supports the premise that components of the framework herein have evolved in practice[34] (though not necessarily as part of a cohesive system) and are effective.   Second, an experienced practitioner stated that while the training only slightly increased his understanding of trial strategy, he found value in that it clarified the ambiguous notions about trial strategy he had amassed thus far in his career.[35]   Presumably this clarification will give him greater facility with those applications he knows and perhaps expand their usefulness into applications he had not yet considered.   In any event, though, we see that these practices exist among experienced litigators, if

---

[31]   *See id.* item 4 (maximizing other's friction).

[32]   The portion regarding clarifying discrete elements of the strategic goal. *See id.* question 8.

[33]   *See id.* Referenced Comments, No. 1.

[34]   The technique evolved for the survey respondent, just as it had evolved in the example described in the training package.

[35]   *See id.* Referenced Comments, No. 2.

only in vague and unstudied form—the very shortcoming this book intends to resolve.[36]

The responses from the focus group members who received live training were more enthusiastic than those from the online training. One hundred percent of the participants intend to use the system (primitive as it then was) in their future practice (37.5% expect to use the system as at mental framework while 62.5% intend to physically draft their plans of action in accordance with the framework).[37] One hundred percent expect the system will improve their performance (37.5% expect slight improvement, 37.5% expect noticeable improvement, and 25% expect a vast improvement).[38] One-hundred percent of the participants also felt the training increased their understanding of the competitive interaction at trial.[39] Notably, one hundred percent also felt the material would be useful to them in pursuing goals outside of trial practice.[40] These results are depicted in Figure 4.

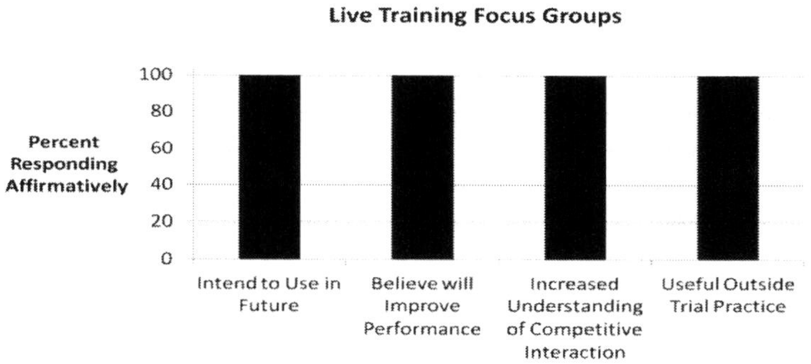

Live Training Focus Groups

Figure 4: Selected Live Focus Group Survey Results

---

[36] While the survey failed to capture the percentage that were already aware of some techniques and which ones, the finding mirrors Neumann's (and Schon's) assertion that strategic processes are "muted" and hidden by labels like wisdom and intuition. *See* Neumann, *supra* note 9.

[37] *See infra* Appendix A, part I. Live Presentation Survey Data, question 7.

[38] *See id.* question 11.

[39] *See id.* question 2.

[40] *See id.* question 3.

While the fully developed framework offered below has not been tested in its final form, the rough cut version demonstrated clear value to the majority of the focus group participants and will be used, in whole or in part, by nearly all of them. Further, the comments from respondents regarding techniques they had already developed (or stumbled upon) demonstrated the value of those as stand-alone techniques.

The mock trial competition provided a different type of validation. The UVA Law School's Mock Trial Team allowed me to work with a group of four first-year law students (in their third month of law school) who had two weeks to prepare for a competition[41] in which they would compete against teams of second- and third-year students[42] who were given six weeks to prepare.[43] While the UVA team did not have time to learn the framework, I walked them through the main steps of strategy creation in addition to the other requirements of trial preparation.

After each of their two competition rounds, at least one member of the opposing team offered—unprompted—that the UVA first-year students had presented unique, compelling arguments for which the other team had not prepared.[44] Unfortunately, this was not sufficient to produce victory. Scoring was based on the quality of the opening statement and closing argument, two direct examinations, two cross-examinations, and the students' objections or motions. In short, tactical abilities, not strategic impact, were scored. The judges did not single out the integration of argument or examinations into the larger case presented.[45] The UVA

---

[41] *See supra* note 266.

[42] Students from the law schools of Emory University and the University of Mississippi.

[43] These factors were not designed to improve the evaluation of this framework; they were simply the situation as it presented.

[44] Score sheets are on file with the author. The comments were stated in the presence of the author and the UVA team members (e-mails confirming this are on file with the author). The other teams seemed additionally genuinely surprised to learn that the UVA team was composed entirely of first year students who had been given limited time to prepare.

[45] For example, the closing argument presented by one competitor received a high score and well-deserved praise for the startling eloquence, clarity, and charm of its poised and engaging presenter, yet the score did not reflect, and no mention was made of the fact, that its well-delivered content never addressed the actual

plaintiff team lost 153–182 and the defense team lost 197–172. While these were less than ideal circumstances to evaluate a strategic framework, the production of unexpected, viable arguments against opponents with greater experience and more preparation time demonstrates that even novices can strategically surprise more skillful tacticians.

In a real trial, likewise, this team of tactical novices would likely have lost. They lacked the tactical skill to press home the advantage created by their surprise, to pin hostile witnesses to prior disadvantageous statements, and to turn ill-shaped testimony into the winning closing argument they envisioned. While strategy may generate success against skilled adversaries with sound cases (as it did for the author in roughly 95% of his cases), the success of any strategy still rests upon a foundation of tactical skill.[46] In short, if one knows strategy and tactics, he can beat others who rely upon tactics alone or who have inferior strategies (reference the Sun Tzu quote at the opening of this chapter). If one lacks tactical ability, however, he will be severely disadvantaged in executing any strategy, no matter how successful the strategy might have proven in the hands of a more capable tactician.[47] This article will revisit strategy's reliance upon tactics below.

In sum, as a proof of concept for this framework, this book offers the research and proven practice of other fields; the focus groups' statistical and anecdotal perceptions of the system's efficacy; the author's record of success while using the underlying principles; and the results of the mock trial competition. This article does not rely upon the outcome of the trial in the following case study[48] although the strategy did result in overwhelming

---

argument advanced by UVA. (Again, score sheets are on file with the author. The comments were stated in the presence of the author and the UVA team members. E-mails confirming this are on file with the author).

[46] Actual trials do not score based upon the attorney's facility with tactics, of course.

[47] The complete version of the Sun Tzu quote from the opening of the chapter is "Strategy without tactics is the slowest route to victory. Tactics without strategy is the noise before defeat." Gentile, *supra* note 2.

[48] It is not offered as a proof of concept for the following reasons: one case is not an adequate sample; the framework as now completed is being retroactively applied to a more rudimentary understanding of the concepts; and the defense attorneys, while fully competent, made many decisions that happened to play into the government's design and suffered bad luck with regard to several factors outside of their control, making the defense appear to be less of an obstacle than one hopes to

success. The case study is instead offered as a clear, succinct source for most of the examples that will be presented to clarify various aspects of the framework throughout this article.

B.   A Case Study[49]

This fact pattern is detailed to the extent necessary to build the coming examples; time spent reading it should pay ample dividends.

1.   The Incident

Mrs. V was in her early twenties and married to a Marine Corps sergeant. One night while her husband was on duty, Mrs. V spent the evening watching a movie with the family of a female friend who lived next door to her. When they finished eating the snacks on hand, her friend's husband, Defendant, went to Mrs. V's house to retrieve some potato chips from her kitchen. After the movies, Mrs. V returned to her empty house, dead bolted her door, and went to sleep.

She awoke later with a start—there was a man crouched at her bedside, touching her in an intimate way. She realized that it was Defendant and began screaming. He fled her bedroom, then her house, leaving her front door open behind him.

The military police (MPs) responded and listened to her story, noting that the potato chips from earlier in the evening were now just inside her front door, and that her other doors and windows were locked. Nothing was stolen and there were no signs of vandalism or forced entry. There was only the unlocked and open front door, which Mrs. V assured the police she had locked before going to bed. The absence of forced entry at the door was significant because Defendant never had access to a key to Mrs. V's front door, nor was he a master locksmith, which is what it would have taken to circumvent her well-made deadbolt.

---

see in a true proof of concept. None of this, however, prevents the case from illustrating concepts, even if it does not sufficiently test their value.

[49] Parties' names have been redacted as a privacy consideration and factual nuances from the situation and especially from the actual trial have been omitted as not relevant to the present discussion.

The MPs next took Defendant's story. He explained that while tidying his house after the movies, he decided to return Mrs. V's leftover potato chips. He found her front door open, was worried because he knew her husband was on duty, so after calling out for her and getting no response, he went inside to check on her. He told the police that he yelled for her several more times inside, and then knocked on the master bedroom door, calling out again.

He figured the knocking and calling must have pulled Mrs. V from a deep sleep because when he stepped into the room, he claimed, she sat up in the bed and started screaming for no apparent reason. He tried to calm her down, but finally decided his presence was making the situation worse. So, he left.

The case went to the government and defense counsel as a proverbial he-said/she-said. Both sides expected that the credibility of each party would ultimately determine the outcome. Before the trial, the defense attacked Mrs. V's credibility by focusing on her insistence that she had locked her front door. They emphasized that Defendant could not have gotten inside without breaking something if the door had actually been locked. As nothing was damaged, clearly neither Defendant nor anyone else broke in. Therefore, despite her claims to the contrary, Mrs. V must have left her front door unlocked. When Mrs. V claims she locked the door—the defense argued—she is either confused about what she did (as she is about everything else that night) or she is lying.

2.   The Trial

During the direct examination of Mrs. V at the actual trial, while the prosecutor had her describe the events of the evening, the defense confidently waited to rise and demonstrate for the jury that Mrs. V is, at the core, baffled and unreliable. *At that moment*, the defense believed they held the initiative, that they would steer the attack while the government defended Mrs. V and attempted damage control.

Then the direct exam took an unexpected turn. The prosecutor had quietly foreshadowed his theory of the case twice. First, he had Mrs. V confirm that she did not habitually check the locks on all the doors and windows in her house (the ones, aside from the front door, which the police had confirmed were locked when they arrived). These other doors and windows were rarely used, and so she did not check them upon returning home the night she was assaulted. Second, when describing the layout of her home, Mrs. V confirmed that her kitchen, where Defendant

15

had gone to get her potato chips, offered a direct view of the home's back door.

Some of the jurors, who of course were not involved in the investigation's fixation on the front door being open when the MPs arrived, pieced this dispersed data together. Those who had been involved in the situation more deeply (i.e., the defense counsel and Mrs. V) remained focused on Defendant entering through the front door and so considered the back door, found locked by the police, to be irrelevant.

Government counsel finally clarified his theory of the case: when Defendant retrieved the potato chips from Mrs. V's house during the movie, Defendant had unlocked Mrs. V's back door. After Mrs. V had returned home and locked her front door, Defendant came in through the back door, locked it, and then opened the front door, where he set the potato chips down as if he had just entered. With his alibi in place, he then entered the master bedroom to attempt a liaison with Mrs. V.[50]

Mrs. V came to understand how she had been set up with a visibly emotional reaction. Her surprise was authentic, as was her fleeting malevolent glance at Defendant. The jurors saw her reaction and it likely reinforced the theory of the case most of them had pieced together for themselves before the prosecutor stated it explicitly. What they had deduced, and the reaction they witnessed, left them invested in the prosecutor's theory of the situation.[51] It fit their view of the situation; it

---

[50] The defense counsel likely overlooked the back door because the investigation had focused on the front door, which was unlocked and was where Defendant had left the potato chips. Also, the case involved a number of charges related to separate incidents (some of which will be discussed *infra*), which produced a mass of information for the attorneys to sort through. Since the MPs found the other doors and windows locked, the back door had faded from scrutiny amid the volumes of discovery, or was disregarded through confirmation bias (the mind's tendency to minimize or disregard information that does not match expectations). *See, e.g.*, Raymond S. Nickerson, *Confirmation Bias: A Ubiquitous Phenomenon in Many Guises* 2(2) REV. OF GEN. PSYCHOL. 175-220 (1998).

[51] The first factor at play is the anchoring bias (because it tethers the mind to a belief). *See, e.g.*, Kenneth E. Hart, David M. Ledgerwood & Phillip A. Ianni, *Applying Social Psychology to Clinical and Counseling Psychology*, *in* APPLIED SOCIAL PSYCHOLOGY 107 (Frank W. Schneider, Jamie A Gruman & Larry M. Coutts, eds., 2nd ed. 2012). It is related to confirmation bias. *See, e.g.*, Nickerson *supra* note 50, at 175–220.

was now their own.[52] The defense would ultimately find it impossible to shake or shift this anchor. They could not, however, simply capitulate.[53]

In assessing the situations, the defense counsel's first thought was likely that it would be pointless to now attack Mrs. V's claim that she locked her front door. Her renewed anger toward Defendant replaced the confusion she had displayed before. Credibility (and specifically, the lack of it seemingly demonstrated by Mrs. V's confusion) was the central issue in the defense theory of the case, but in the contest of credibility, Mrs. V now stood far ahead the Defendant. The defense theory was torpedoed.

A second concern likely struck the defense counsel then: the nature of the case had changed. They walked into the courtroom prepared to defend what appeared to be—at worst—a crime of opportunity. The point of conflict had been whether Mrs. V had imagined Defendant touching her. Defendant's entry of the home was plausibly explained by a tired woman not fully latching her door (perhaps followed by a light breeze or gravity gradually opening it wider), and Defendant's legitimate concern.

Now, however, the case held the specter of premeditation. Defendant had the opportunity to pre-arrange his entry hours before the alleged offense. The immediate point of conflict just shifted from her perception to how Defendant entered the home.

With the prosecutor sitting down, the lead defense counsel needed to begin his cross-examination... yet he remained seated. He had been

---

[52] The second factor at play is self esteem. The idea the person has anchored to is not just a random belief; it is one they arrived at through their own work, thus pride is involved. *See, e.g.*, Joshua Klayman *Varieties of Confirmation Bias*, DECISION MAKING FROM A COGNITIVE PERSPECTIVE 408 (Jerome R. Busemeyer ed. 1995).

[53] The failure to dust for fingerprints at the back door provided an opportunity for the standard defense argument that the investigation was shoddy, a point the prosecutor anticipated. He came prepared to focus on the fact that Mrs. V very credibly affirmed that she locked her front door, and the government did not need to prove that Defendant managed to get inside; Defendant had already admitted to the police that he was inside. The failure to fingerprint did not excuse or explain Defendant's entry and made his explanation of what happened in the bedroom dubious. Perhaps anticipating that attacking the lack of fingerprints would simply prolong the jury's focus on Mrs. V's insistence that she locked her door, and the weakness of their claim that he found the front door standing open, the defense did not raise the shoddy investigation argument.

comfortably on the offensive moments earlier. Now his case lay in disarray and his client's credibility under siege—the prosecutor had not just seized the initiative from him, in a single stroke the government had completely reversed the situation.[54] The defense could request a recess, but that would give time for Mrs. V's testimony to cement in the juror's minds, and it would make the defense look weak to the jury of Marines, as if they needed to regroup. Facing two equally unappealing options, the defense was in a textbook-style dilemma; there was no "right" answer, no accessible positive result.[55] Further, the defense appeared too unsettled to even determine which option was less damaging. Better planning and strategy could have saved their case, but while they had planned—extensively—their planning had not been effective. The prosecution's planning, on the other hand, was rapidly proving to be decisive.

C. The Strategic System

We will revisit the case study throughout the coming pages as we build a way of thinking about strategy and a method for effective production of

---

[54] "The expert in battle moves the enemy and is not moved by him." SUN TZU *supra* note 17, at 123. The prosecutor's move, one known as "stealing a tempo," nears the acme of moving and not being moved by the opponent, describing a situation more expansive, yet more focused, than simply "seizing the initiative." Rather than first negating the opponent's offense (move 1), then taking an offensive action (move 2), both acts are accomplished in a single stroke, responding in a way that forces the opponent to take defensive action. *See, e.g.,* YASSER SEIRAWAN & JEREMY SILMAN, WINNING CHESS TACTICS 225 (1995). While the term is derived from chess, it has previously been applied to litigation, if only in fiction. HILLARY WAUGH, PARRISH FOR THE DEFENSE 122 (1974).

[55] This highlights the difference between the mock trial team's use of strategy and the prosecutor's. The prosecutor's execution made the strategic problem he created for the defense inescapable. Alternatively, when the opponent has a possibility of escape, the attorney must be poised to exploit the dilemma he creates, to counter the opponent's reactive attempts to wriggle free. *See infra* Chapter 5, part A. In contrast to the government action here, while the mock trial team successfully presented a problem, their situation lacked the tactical shock achieved here. Nor did the mock trial team's level of experience allow them to add additional problems and exploit the lesser level of disruption they did achieve. *See id.* This is in no way a slight on the mock trial team. Few if any students in the first months of law school have the tactical depth to create decisive effects; the two weeks they were given to prepare (amid a standard first-year course load) was not going to provide them the needed depth. As noted above, strategy is limited by tactical skill.

strategies. Chapter 2 introduces the strategic philosophy of maneuver and its central framework, the OODA Loop. The OODA Loop describes the mental process of an individual in a conflict—they observe changes, orient (determining what the change means and what they can do about it), make a decision about what to do next, and then act. In maneuver, the goal is to get through the process as quickly as one is able while also possibly denying adversaries the opportunity to do the same.

The force that interferes with progress through the OODA Loop is called "friction." Friction is the subject of Chapter 3, and the final foundational element we need discuss. With the foundation complete we will delineate a method for proceeding through litigation with a fast, compact OODA Loop, understanding and being prepared for the variety of attacks an adversary may offer.

Chapter 4 discusses how a tight, fast Loop is the result of preparation and adaptation. We will see how these can be achieved using a Line of Operations, as outlined in the left column of Figure 2, supra.

Chapter 5 will discuss how adversaries attempt to affect our actions, as depicted in the right-hand column of Figure 2. Chapter 6, the conclusion, integrates the prior sections and highlights how the framework herein can produce a comprehensive, properly-sequenced, plan with focused, integrated, mutually-supportive actions that have a reasonable probability of success, are capable of rapid adaptation to new circumstances, increasing the number of perceptible opportunities, and of shaping adversaries' actions to ensure the attorney achieves his overarching purpose. Moreover, this framework can be developed and communicated to support the instruction of future trial advocates in the skills of litigation strategy. The description of this system will begin with a survey of the maneuver philosophy of conflict.

2 ➤ MANEUVER PHILOSOPHY

One method of trial practice is the direct approach: arguing the facts or the law, presenting stronger arguments or marshalling better evidence. The other approach is indirect—avoiding direct confrontations of evidence or arguments by, for instance, introducing red herrings and straw men.[56] Like red herrings and straw men, maneuver is an indirect philosophy; however one more refined, more comprehensive, and more ambitious than these indirect approaches common to litigation. Rather than merely presenting diversions, maneuver "seeks to shatter the enemy's cohesion through a variety of rapid, focused, and unexpected actions which create a turbulent and rapidly deteriorating situation with which the enemy cannot cope."[57]

Maneuver in litigation does not attack arguments or evidence conventionally; it targets an opponent's ability to function.[58] The case study presented an example of this. The prosecution pre-empted an argument

---

[56] *See, e.g.*, PAUL BOSANAC, LITIGATION LOGIC 379 – 406 (2009) (This American Bar Association publication devotes one chapter each to the use of red herrings and straw men in litigation.).

[57] U.S. MARINE CORPS, MARINE CORPS REFERENCE PUB. (MCRP) 5-12C, MARINE CORPS SUPPLEMENT TO THE DOD DICTIONARY OF MILITARY AND ASSOCIATED TERMS, at II-38 (2011) [hereinafter MCRP 5-12C].

[58] *C.f.* ADMIRAL WILLIAM A. OWENS & EDWARD OFFLEY, LIFTING THE FOG OF WAR 137 (2000) ("In maneuver warfare the assumption is that there are significant differences among military targets, and that some have more value than others because their destruction will have a more severe impact on the enemy's ability to function").

over whether Mrs. V locked her front door by unexpectedly demonstrating how Defendant might have entered through the back. This caused the defense multiple unanticipated problems and undercut the defense's central theme, that Mrs. V was unreliable. The prosecution created a situation that made it difficult for the defense to respond intelligently to the new issue of premeditation, or to produce a replacement for their newly-hollowed theory of the case.[59] Because maneuver does not rely primarily upon evidence or argument, it allows the poorly-resourced but creative attorney to level the playing field against attorneys with more financing and more favorable evidence at the same time it prepares them to defend against such attacks.

The core of the maneuver philosophy is the OODA Loop. The dislocation sought in maneuver is achieved by taking intelligent actions (i.e., "focused, unexpected actions"[60]) faster than an opponent can respond to them. These actions, and the adversary's reactions, are the last step (the "A") in each attorney's respective OODA Loop. When an attorney is acting—shaping the landscape and controlling the flow of events—his opponent is generally responding and not reshaping the situation. Opponents who are reacting are limited in their ability to create problems for the attorney. Action is the key, and the key to producing intelligent action is to speed and tighten one's own Loop. In addition to tightening his own operations to facilitate speed, the attorney will want to understand how an opponent may attempt to unnaturally expand his Loop. Whether seeking speed or wishing to remain impervious to attacks, the attorney must understand the nature of the OODA Loop.

As noted above, "OODA" is an acronym for Observe, Orient, Decide, Act.[61] When an event occurs, an attorney must first "observe" it (for OODA purposes, this includes hearing and other forms of sensory input, not just visual observation). Next he orients, trying to figure out *what it means* (putting it in context, determining related implications) and *what he can do about it.*[62] Then he decides on a course of action and, finally, he acts,

---

[59] *C.f.* LIND *supra* note 21, at 7 ("Maneuver warfare means you will not only accept confusion and disorder and operate successfully within it. . . . [Y]ou will also *generate* confusion and disorder.") (emphasis in original).

[60] MCRP 5-12C, *supra* note 57, at II-38.

[61] *See supra* Figure 1.

[62] *See* Richard Breton & Robert Rousseau, *The Analysis of Team Decision Making Architectures*, DECISION MAKING IN COMPLEX ENVIRONMENTS 243 (Malcolm Cook, Jan Noyes & Yvonne Masakowski eds. 2007) ("The goal with the OODA

executing the chosen response. The process repeats as he observes the effects of his action and decides what to do from there.

In a given period of time, depending on the number of issues that require attention, an attorney will be running through a number of loops, and on more than one level. First, the overarching planning effort can be considered one prolonged OODA Loop.[63] Planning starts by looking at the situation and the client's goals: observation. The attorney then analyzes the significance of elements and places them into context with each other (orienting) before devising and analyzing his possible actions. He will eventually decide upon and pursue one of those courses of action. Finally, he will act, completing one drawn-out, planning-level OODA sequence.[64]

Throughout the course of this big, strategic OODA Loop, the attorney will be dealing with minor issues and individual events. He will be making observations and considering actions, perhaps puzzling out an odd remark by opposing counsel or considering how to exploit a witness's word choice. These minor, individual tasks will have two effects. First, they require the attorney to reassess and possibly adapt his plan (his overarching Loop). Even if no action is necessary, he must still spend time updating his mental picture of the situation, orienting the new information in the context of his plan. Second, any significant shifts (any new potential obstacles or opportunities, such as the witness's unexpected word choice) require individual attention, and possibly some action that will reverse or exploit

---

phases is to reduce as much as possible the uncertainty in the situation within the time constraints in order to select the most appropriate course of action.").

[63] All planning processes proceed along similar paths, so the terminology attached to the planning system is immaterial. Every party in a competitive environment will take steps to assimilate information and deal with obstacles. Here I continue using the terms of the OODA Loop so as not to overload the reader with additional jargon. The reader should feel free, if he or she feels it will be beneficial, to substitute the jargon of whatever planning or problem solving process he is familiar with. The conclusion below, that introducing more problems makes it more difficult for the person to comprehend the situation and achieve beneficial results, will be identical.

[64] *See generally* U.S. DEP'T OF THE ARMY, FIELD MANUAL (FM) 5-0, THE OPERATIONS PROCESS (2010); U.S. MARINE CORPS, MARINE CORPS WARFIGHTING PUBLICATION (MCWP) 5-1, MARINE CORPS PLANNING PROCESS (2010); WESLEY B. TRUITT, BUSINESS PLANNING: A COMPREHENSIVE FRAMEWORK AND PROCESS (2002).

whatever just happened. Such individual responses require specific consideration—the processing of a mini-OODA Loop.

Consider the opening case study. As the prosecutor first revealed his theory that Defendant entered through the back door (provoking the emotional reaction from Mrs. V), the defense counsel was likely thinking that the victim's credibility had increased and that the thrust of his planned cross-examination (that Defendant could not—and would not—have gotten inside if Mrs. V had actually locked her door) would be dead on arrival. Here the defense counsel is working on one sub-Loop about the victim's credibility. But in the middle of orienting on the credibility issue, he realizes that the prosecution has suggested that Defendant opened the back door long before the assault—this implies premeditation, and so the defense counsel begins a second sub-Loop before coming to any conclusion on the first. He now has two incomplete sub-Loops. Figure 5, *infra*, depicts the various Loops an attorney may be processing at a given time.

Ideally, information gained through processing the minor issues will feed into the attorney's running assessment—his view of the overall situation—but it may merely distract him from it; this is reflected in the arrows between the sub-Loops to the overarching Loop.

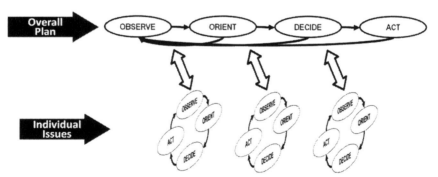

Figure 5: Individual Issues (sub-Loops) Feeding and Distracting from the Overarching Plan

While one's strategy should focus on the jurors' perception of the facts (as their perceptions generally determine the verdict), maneuver largely uses the OODA Loop to addresses the attorney's relationship with opponents. The intent of this use is to "collapse [the] adversary's system into *confusion* and *disorder* by causing him to over and under react to activity that appears simultaneously *menacing* as well as *ambiguous, chaotic,* or *misleading.*"[65]

The collection of forces causing confusion and disorder, interfering with forward progress through the OODA Loop are called "friction."[66] An attorney can reduce his level of friction, and move more quickly through his OODA Loop, by planning properly, and by adapting rapidly to changes (as noted in Figure 2, *supra*). Similarly, by creating friction opponents will attempt to expand or disrupt your OODA Loop.[67] So, whether an attorney desires to tighten his own OODA Loop to out-pace his opponent and take control of events, or to adapt rapidly and overcome difficulties created by those adversaries, he must understand friction.

---

[65] OSINGA *supra* note 15, at 141 (citing John Boyd; emphasis in original). Note that while one wants to mislead or create ambiguity for his opponent he, of course, must avoid confusing the jury.

[66] CARL VON CLAUSEWITZ, ON WAR 119 (1976) (Michael Howard & Peter Paret eds., trans.) (Book 1, chapter 7 for other translations).

[67] *See, e.g.,* OSINGA *supra* note 15, at 141.

3 ➤ FRICTION

Everything in war is very simple, but the simplest thing is difficult. The difficulties accumulate and end by producing a kind of friction that is inconceivable unless one has experienced war.[68]

Friction may be mental, as [with] indecision over a course of action. . . . Friction may be external, imposed by enemy action ... or mere chance. Friction may be self-induced, caused by such factors as lack of a clearly defined goal, lack of coordination, unclear or complicated plans[69]

Friction encompasses all of the forces that hinder a person as he attempts to take effective action, however, this book will focus only on the primary sources of friction: the "dancing landscape"[70] (the array of shifting,

---

[68] CLAUSEWITZ, *supra* note 666, at 119 (Book 1, chapter 7 for other translations).

[69] U.S. MARINE CORPS, MARINE CORPS DOCTRINAL PUBLICATION (MCDP) 1, WARFIGHTING at 5-6 (1997).

[70] Charles M. Gastle & Susan Boughs, *Microsoft III and the Metes and Bounds of Software Design and Technological Tying Doctrine*, 6 VA.J.L.& TECH. 7 (2001)(" [A] dancing landscape . . . has a constantly changing topography. This occurs because the factors that describe the landscape are constantly fluctuating").

interconnected variables that affect our situation), fog (inaccurate, misinterpreted, or missing information),[71] and other parties.[72]

A. The Dancing Landscape

The strategic landscape is composed of all the variables that will affect the outcome of a trial. In the case study, the central variables that would decide the outcome were the jurors' perceptions of Mrs. V's and Defendant's credibility. These two variables, however, would be affected by a host of other variables—the testimony of military policemen, argument of counsel, the testimony of Mrs. V and of Defendant, and so on. These interconnected variables form the strategic landscape on which the defense and government counsel pursued their verdict.

While geographic landscapes generally remain still, strategic landscapes will shift, or "dance," as different parties take action.[73] This causes variables (such as the juror's perception of Defendant's credibility) to change as witnesses and counsel make statements, introduce evidence, and present arguments.

Actions and responses can create unexpected results, as when a witness remembers something new or forgets what he earlier claimed to have seen, or when opposing counsel introduces new problems (like Defendant's entry

---

[71] *See, e.g.*, OWENS & OFFLEY *supra* note 58, at 12 ("[T]he fog of war would always be there, always cloaking and hiding what was actually taking place.").

[72] While these are the primary sources, this list is not exhaustive, nor is it a full exploration of the concept of stress. Though Clausewitz coined the term "friction," the best descriptors of its difficulty-magnifying property were independently arrived at in the forms of Field Theory and Dancing Landscapes. Clausewitz, for his part, cited three sources of friction: fog (a topic we will address shortly), emotion, and interaction (the fact that your actions cause others to act). *See* CLAUSEWITZ, *supra* note 66, at 137-40. Field theory comes from psychology. *See generally* KURT LEWIN, FIELD THEORY IN SOCIAL SCIENCE (1951). Dancing landscapes arose in complexity theory. *See, e.g.*, SCOTT E. PAGE, DIVERSITY AND COMPLEXITY 157 (2011).

[73] *See, e.g.*, Desmond Ng, *Supply Chain Organization through Entrepreneurship and Management of Knowledge Networks, in* PARADOXES IN FOOD CHAINS AND NETWORKS 346 (J.H. Trienekens, S.W.F. Omta eds. 2002) ("Organizations are said to be continually adjusting to the demands of others and thus are adapting on a "dancing landscape"").

through the back door). Unexpected changes, or expected ones for which the attorney was nonetheless unprepared, create friction. Those who wish to remain competitive on such a landscape must adapt, and preferably rapidly, before further changes occur. Even with rapid adaptation, though, an attorney cannot hope to optimize every variable and get the absolute best result at every turn. What he can do is try to identify the variables he can control, and predict the coming movements of those he cannot, so that he can prevent them from interfering with his plans.

In order to predict what will occur—prediction being a necessary precursor to timely, intelligent adaptation[74]—we must understand our situation—we must have a sufficient level of situational awareness. And situational awareness brings us to the source of friction known as "fog."

B. Fog

> *If we know where we are and something about how we got there, we might see where we are trending—and if the outcomes which lie naturally in our course are unacceptable, to make timely change.*[75]

> *[T]he deliberate cultivation of uncertainty and mistakenness by one party in the mind of the other are of the essence*[76]

---

[74] OSINGA, *supra* note 15, at 27 (Other factors, like fast transitions from one maneuver to the next and fast tempo support the central guidance that "[h]e who can handle the quickest rate of change survives"). Information plays a key role in adapting and surviving in competition. Network-Centric Warfare, for example, devotes much effort to minimizing information asymmetry within an organization, using modern C4I (Command, Control, Communications, Computers and Intelligence) to spread information from the highest to lowest levels in the combat force, thereby reducing the adversary's information advantages. *See, e.g.*, PAUL T. MITCHELL, NETWORK CENTRIC WARFARE AND COALITION OPERATIONS 99 (2009)

[75] FRED R. DAVID, STRATEGIC MANAGEMENT, 11TH ED., 3 (2007) (quoting Abraham Lincoln.)

[76] ALAN CODDINGTON & G.L.S. SHACKLE, THEORIES OF THE BARGAINING PROCESS vii (1968)

Fog, as a strategic term, denotes information issues: you do not have all the information you want[77] and some information you do have is ambiguous; some of the information you think you know turns out to be wrong or directly contradicts some other fact you "know"; and then there is information that you simply have no inkling of that will result in you being surprised, if not totally blindsided. Because these information issues prevent one from clearly "seeing" the situation, they are called "fog."[78] Fog is a source of friction because quick and clear observations are essential for actions to be timely and intelligent.

Ideally, one wants to understand a situation *before* it unfolds, so that he can prepare. Accurate predictions prevent an attorney from being surprised (as happened to the defense in the opening case study). Preparation, which in the context of "fog" includes thoroughly and properly analyzing the situation, enables faster more effective *adaptation* to events the attorney was unable to predict.[79] Prediction creates greater information demands than adaptation. Adaptation only requires the attorney to observe a single outcome after it has unfolded, while prediction requires the attorney to understand every factor affecting the outcome he is concerned with (to include knowing how his adversary and others will act as events unfold).

---

[77] This encompasses the issues identified in game theory as incomplete and imperfect information. To greatly simplify, imperfect information is unknown actions, incomplete information regards unknown motives. An attorney's information is imperfect when he does not know if the opposing counsel has prepared a witness for the points he intends to attack. Information is incomplete when an attorney does not know why the opposing party has demanded certain terms of a settlement or how they will respond to his actions. These two categories are specifically identified from among the broader array of information issues because they prevent an attorney from accurately assessing the value of the different actions he might take, . *See, e.g.,* HANS PETERS, GAME THEORY, A MULTI-LEVELED APPROACH 59 (2008)

[78] The absence and unreliability of information causes events to take place "in a kind of twilight . . . like fog or moonlight." CLAUSEWITZ *supra* note 66, at 140. This is popularly known as "the fog of war," but this fog is equally applicable to litigation. A general description of sources of "fog" (primarily referencing business situations), and the problems and advantages that arise with information asymmetry is available in *Co-opetition. See* BRANDENBURGER & NALEBUFF, *supra* note 233, at 198–227.

[79] *See infra* Chapter 4.

Unfortunately, the trial environment is naturally opposed to quick, clear observations. Almost all information comes to an attorney through the filter of investigators, witnesses, or one of the other parties involved, all of whom are subject to misperceptions, miscalculations, and other cognitive errors.[80] Such filters, moreover, do not prevent attorneys from confronting a deluge of information.[81] Extracting relevant data from the flood is difficult (we saw this in the case study with the defense counsel failing to note the back door as a possible point of entry despite having access to all the requisite facts). Once relevant information is extracted, its meaning may still be false, in conflict with other information, or it might be ambiguous in some other way.[82] In short, information overload compounds the fog.

Then there is information asymmetry. Some of the information an attorney lacks will be known to others, and he (hopefully) will know things that others do not.[83] This imbalance extends beyond *possessing* specific pieces of information to *perceptions* of the information—understanding the meaning, the accuracy, and the significance of the information in every relevant context.[84] The case study demonstrated how, even after the prosecutor referred to the back door of Mrs. V's house (singling it out from the flood of data for special, if only momentary, consideration), the defense team apparently failed to perceive its relevance as a possible point of entry.

---

[80] *See, e.g.,* Vincent S. Walkowiak, *Preserving Candor Between Lawyers and Clients, in* THE ATTORNEY-CLIENT PRIVILEGE IN CIVIL LITIGATION 123-46 (2008) (discusses the need to extract information from clients, "warts and all").

[81] *See, e.g.,* Ruth Bird, *Legal Information Literacy, in* The IALL Intenational Handbook of Legal Information Management 115 (2011) (discussing information overload in the legal profession).

[82] For example, pursuing a plea or settlement agreement could mean that my client would prefer not to go to trial, or it could be a means of eliciting information ("screening," in game theory terms) or stalling for time to improve his position or develop the situation. Accepting the agreement, however, is unambiguous. My client would not accept it if he felt he would receive a better result through trial.

[83] The rules of privilege and work product virtually guarantee imbalances in the information attorneys will hold. *See, e.g.,* MANUAL FOR COURTS-MARTIAL, UNITED STATES, (MCM) MIL. R. EVID. 501 – 504.

[84] *See infra* Chapter 5, part B. The "orient" phase of the OODA Loop is analyzed. Note in particular Figure 15.

At this point there was an imbalance in the perceptions of the back door between the opposing counsel, and even between some of the jurors and the defense team. Because perceptions are shaped by personal factors such as education, experience, and cultural values, as well as by expectations and emotions at the moment the party is processing the information,[85] there will always be imbalances in perception that extend beyond the asymmetry in information held.[86]

Information asymmetry and differing perceptions affect the "orientation" phase of the OODA Loop, and can be used to create surprise,[87] disrupting your OODA Loop, rendering you ineffective for a time (again, consider the case study) or —when the surprise is more mild— simply catch you unprepared to address a problem that requires immediate attention. Understanding the potential problems of "fog," we can see the need for accurate predictions, and for having accurate points of reference when things do surprise us. An invaluable tool for prediction is utility theory, and the most effective guidepost is the concept of "purpose." Utility and purpose are interrelated, so we will examine these topics together now.

C. Purpose and Utility

> *"Would you tell me, please, which way I ought to go from here?"*
> *"That depends a good deal on where you want to get to," said the Cat.*
> *"I don't much care where—" said Alice.*
> *"Then it doesn't matter which way you go," said the Cat.*
> *"—so long as I get somewhere," Alice added as an explanation.*
> *"Oh, you're sure to do that," said the Cat, "if you only walk long enough."[88]*

Strategy exists to achieve goals[89] so, not surprisingly, "objective"

---

[85] *Id.*

[86] *Id.*

[87] *See infra* Chapter 5, part B.

[88] LEWIS CARROLL, ALICE'S ADVENTURES IN WONDERLAND 47 (1865)

appears among the listed strategic principles in the doctrine of most major military forces in the world.[90] Because the final objective—and not how we get there—is the overriding concern, we can remain unconcerned with the course events take so long as they arrive at the desired destination, achieving the criteria of success. As obstacles appear, one can remove them or go around them or choose an entirely new route, so long as the goal is achieved.[91] There are many paths to most every destination, and that destination, the purpose, is our concern. Strategy's focus upon purpose leads to the following requirements of the strategic system herein:

1. Be clear in your purpose.[92] Know the measures of success and failure; know as specifically as possible where the line between them lies;

2. Remain focused on your purpose (not straying after other goals without considered justification);[93]

3. Have as clear a picture as possible of every requirement along the path to achieving it;[94] and

---

[89] Strategy is "the art of devising or employing plans or stratagems *toward a goal*" (emphasis added). WEBSTERS NINTH NEW COLLEGIATE DICTIONARY 1165 (1985).

[90] General Donn A. Starry, *The Principles of War*, 61(9) MIL. REV. 6 (Sept, 1981).

[91] This should not be read as advocating that "the end justifies the means." This book has already noted the need for ethics to be applied in tandem with strategy. Furthermore, ethics often play a role in shaping the end. As I revise this text, the legacy of Joe Paterno as a football coach has been vacated because he failed to report the alleged sexual assaults upon children made by one of his assistant coaches—Paterno's apparent objective (winning games) was rendered moot by his alleged ethical shortcomings.

[92] *See, e.g.*, U. S. DEP'T OF DEFENSE, JOINT PUB. (JP) 5-0, JOINT OPERATION PLANNING, at GL-13 (2006) (Every military operation should be directed toward a clearly defined, decisive and attainable objective).

[93] *See, e.g., id.*

[94] *See, e.g.*, MAO ZEDONG, COLLECTED WRITINGS OF CHAIRMAN MAO VOL II: GUERRILLA WARFARE 161 ("[I]t is necessary for the strategic direction of the war to make a rough sketch of its trends. Although our sketch may not be in full accord with the subsequent facts and will be amended by them, it is still necessary to make it in order to give firm and purposeful strategic direction to the protracted war.").

4. Practice "economy of force": Take only actions which increase your chances of achieving your goal.[95]

These principles are implicit throughout the balance of this book. With them, an attorney can reduce fog (minimize the chance of failing to foresee a possibility) and minimize the effects of the shifting strategic landscape (more quickly adapt to changes in the situation). Additionally, knowing other parties' purposes allows the attorney to predict with some reliability how they will act and react, and to present specifically-tailored decoys to pull them off-course or shape their action.[96]

Within the ambit of "purpose," the concept of "utility" is invaluable in reliably predicting how others will respond to decoys or otherwise pursue their purpose. "Utility" describes the amount of value a person receives from something.[97] It is a measure of their satisfaction, fulfillment or accomplishment. Attorneys and witnesses receive utility from actions that bring them closer to their purpose, and when choosing between different possible courses of action, they generally pursue the one they expect will bring them the greatest amount of utility.[98] Perceived benefits drive action,

---

[95] *C.f.* FM 3-90 *supra* note 188, at 8-16 ("The commander uses economy of force measures in areas that do not involve his decisive operation to mass the effects of his forces in the area where a decision is sought).

[96] *See infra* Chapter 5, part C., Shaping.

[97] *See, e.g.,* FUAD ALESKEROV, DENIS BOUYSSOU & BERNARD MONJARDET, UTILITY MAXIMIZATION, CHOICE AND PREFERENCE 1 (2nd ed. 2007).

[98] *Id. See also, e.g.,* ROBERT H. KLONOFF & PAUL L. COLBY, WINNING JURY TRIALS: TRIAL TACTICS AND SPONSORSHIP STRATEGIES 4-6 (3rd ed. 2007) (citing example of a prosecutor who did not introduce a videotape of a witness identifying the defendant in a line up because the witness's hesitation would have damaged his case; while the defense could not introduce the same tape because it would have been even more damaging to their case—thus each pursued the best benefit (utility) to their case. The text goes on to note that "sponsorship" of evidence—the party that introduces the evidence, making it their own—can shift the benefit. In this same situation, had the government introduced the evidence the defense would have been able to use it to their greater benefit (gaining more utility) by saying the government relied on a tape in which the witness clearly hesitated, demonstrating doubt. Likewise, if the defense had introduced the evidence, the prosecutor could have used it to greater benefit saying the defense was relying on a tape where, in the end, the witness identified the accused with certainty. In this way, the concept of "sponsorship" is based on utility and utility shifting). Utility shifting, applied

so understanding another party's purpose as a primary source of utility allows one to predict with some reliability what that party will do when confronted with a choice. But there are limits to this predictive power, and here is where friction returns.

The overarching purpose is not a party's only possible source of utility. Parties can be distracted from their overarching purpose by new and fleeting goals (for example, seizing an opportunity to embarrass an annoying hostile witness), and they can be hindered by "bounded rationality" (poor thinking, e.g., not understanding which course of action will move them closest to their goal, as the case study depicted with regard to the defense team's quandary about asking for a recess or pressing ahead with the cross-examination of Mrs. V). Additionally, because they do not want their actions predicted, other parties will be devious. They conceal their motives and avoid taking the direct, predictable route to their objective (e.g., if an attorney wants to demonstrate for the jury that a witness is lying, he rarely will simply ask the witness to admit he is a liar). Figure 6 depicts the relationship of purpose and utility with bounded rationality, new and fleeting goals, and deviousness.

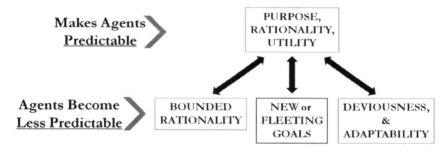

Figure 6: Predictions Based Upon Rationality[99]

---

broadly (without restriction or further reference to sponsorship), is discussed *infra* Chapter 4, part B.1., Validating Courses of Action, and Chapter 5, part C., Shaping.

[99] Bounded rationality creates unpredictability. That is, when a party does not understand events, he may be unable to determine the rational, and therefore predictable, course of action. *C.f.* HERBERT ALEXANDER SIMON, MODELS OF BOUNDED RATIONALITY 234 (1997) ("[U]npredictable shifts in a system reduce the ability of actors to respond rationally."). New goals create new sources of utility, which if not identified are not predictable, rational responses. Jerome R. Busemeyer, James T. Townsend & Julie Stout, *Motivational Underpinnings of Utility in Decision Making*, EMOTIONAL COGNITION 197 (Simon C. Moore & Mike Oaksford eds. 2002) ("needs change over time as a function of external stimulation).

The friction created by deviousness and adaptability can be reduced by viewing all of a party's actions through the context of his purpose. For example, in the case study, the defense knew that the prosecutor had the objective of ensuring Mrs. V was perceived as credible, and faced the obstacle of her insistence that she locked her front door despite the police having found it open. So, when the prosecutor began discussing (deviously out of context) the proximity of Mrs. V's back door to the kitchen where Defendant retrieved the potato chips, the defense could have assessed the relevance of the back door in light of the prosecutor's objective, making Mrs. V appear more credible. A sufficiently agile and determined mind might have then seen how the government could use the back door to address Mrs. V's credibility with regard to her statement about the front door.

In addition to reducing fog by clarifying the true intent of others' ambiguous or deceptive acts, "purpose" can aid in prediction. When preparing for trial and considering various courses of action, we can deduce an adversary's likely response to our actions by considering what a person who valued what they value, whose purpose was their purpose, would do when confronting that situation—the standard walking-in-the-other-person's-shoes method, but one we will refine and enhance below.[100]

The other sources of unpredictability in opponents—bounded rationality and fleeting goals—can also be anticipated, and seemingly ambiguous conduct can be clarified, through understanding a party's purpose and sources of utility.

3. *Bounded Rationality & Fleeting Goals*

Nothing is attained in war except by calculation.[101]

[M]y pride, my anger, my passion is stronger than my calculation.[102]

Individuals engage in deception to increase the likelihood of achieving goals. *See, e.g.,* ROBERT W. MITCHELL & NICHOLAS S. THOMPSON, DECEPTION: PERSPECTIVES ON HUMAN AND NONHUMAN DECEIT 358 (1986). *See also* SUN TZU, ART OF WAR 6 (Lionel Giles trans. 1996) ("Never will those who wage war tire of deception.").

[100] *See infra* Chapter 4, part B.1.

[101] DAVID G. CHANDLER, THE CAMPAIGNS OF NAPOLEON 145 (1966) (quoting a letter from Napoleon to his brother Joseph dated, June 6, 1806).

People are viewed as "rational" when they take actions they think will bring them the greatest possible utility.[103] Napoleon's advocacy of calculation in the quote above is a prescient endorsement of weighing utility. Actions that produce no, or little, discernible utility are deemed "irrational."[104] Utility comes from various sources—from tangible, material gains as well as from emotional benefits. These are the driving forces Euripides alludes to above, with pride, anger, and passion overcoming calculation. Though these forces may distract a person from his long-term goals, they do not render him "irrational" in terms of utility theory if he gains a desired benefit through following his emotions. For instance, a defendant may still be acting rationally even when he is *increasing* his chance of confinement or financial loss, as when he takes pride in refusing to testify against a co-conspirator, or when he continues with a losing law suit for the pleasure of increasing the plaintiff's frustration and expense. Finally, people sometimes hold related-but conflicting-beliefs (an problem called cognitive dissonance). Thus actions that are irrational as to one goal may actually be taken in pursuit of the conflicting goal, having not taken the time to consider the counter-productive outcome as to his main goal.

---

[102] EURIPIDES, MEDEA vers. 1078-1080 (H. Lloyd-Jones trans. 1980).

[103] PAUL WEIRICH, COLLECTIVE RATIONALITY: EQUILIBRIUM IN COOPERATIVE GAMES 31-53 (2009). A possible exception to rationality occurs with "moral hazard," which is when a third party is absorbing the cost, as when an insurance company will pay the defendant's damages, or when the defendant absorbs the cost (in time served or damages paid) for his attorney's mistakes. *See, e.g.*, Prajit K. Dutta & Roy Radner, *Moral Hazard, in* 2 HANDBOOK OF GAME THEORY WITH ECONOMIC APPLICATIONS at 871-73 (Robert Aumann & Sergui Hart eds. 1994). Another factor is diminishing marginal utility. For example, while a defendant would prefer a forty year sentence to a forty five year sentence, the difference in utility of those five years is far less than if he were considering the difference between a one-year vice a six-year sentence. His utility for "five years" diminished as the magnitude of the sentence increased. *See, e.g.*, WARREN F. ILCHMAN & NORMAN THOMAS UPHOFF, THE POLITICAL ECONOMY OF CHANGE 106 (1969).

[104] Being devious, taking indirect measures to achieve goals, when it is believed they increase the likelihood of achieving the goal, is rational. *See, e.g.*, ALESKEROV, BOUYSSOU & MONJARDET, *supra* note 97, at 1. The Theory of Rational Addiction, too, posits that addiction (e.g., smoking though one wants to quit) is rational because the party prioritizes (albeit through compulsion) immediate gratification over the desire to not take the action. *See, e.g.*, ROBERT WEST, AINSLEY HARDY, THEORY OF ADDICTION 32-33 (2006).

This leads to the converse of the point made above: just as an attorney can predict actions by understanding purpose and utility, he can understand a party's immediate purpose and source of utility by observing their actions.

Additionally, the importance and immediacy with which an adversary views his overarching goal can vary as new attractions appear. Some parties will remain steadfast in pursuit of their overarching purpose (an attitude recommended herein), but many will be susceptible to emotional lures such as revenge, ego-building (trying things they think will impress others), or immediate, pressing concerns.[105] Increasing a plaintiff's frustration may suddenly become less important to a defendant whose wife has just announced she plans to leave him. Lying to protect a co-conspirator may become insignificant to an accused about to lose his job or his family's apartment. New priorities arise and the urgency of old ones fades.[106] Remaining focused on one's purpose—deciding consciously whether this new desire deserves to override the purpose of the strategy—should aid the attorney in overcoming the distractions he will confront (and help him to avoid issues like "mission creep"[107] and "strategic drift"[108]).

When it is another party distracted by chance events, an attorney may have to confront unpredicted, seemingly irrational actions ("seemingly" because he does not immediately know what goal is driving them). While there is no cure for others' random distractions, effective planning should

---

[105] *See, e.g., id. See also* MARK A.R. KLEIMAN, WHEN BRUTE FORCE FAILS 1-2 (2009) (The distant prospect of punishment is outweighed by the immediacy of enjoying the fruit of the crime).

[106] *See, e.g.,* WEST & HARDY *supra* note 104, at 32-33.

[107] "Mission creep" is an issue of goals pulling a party away from their original purpose: "the incremental addition of a series of new requirements each of which is a reasonable step by itself but that together produce an unreasonable aggregate result." MICHAEL J. NORTH & CHARLES M. MACAL, MANAGING BUSINESS COMPLEXITY: DISCOVERING STRATEGIC SOLUTIONS WITH OTHER BASED MODELING AND SIMULATION 284 (2007). The party sets additional goals as events unfold without weighing their feasibility in relation to the others and de-conflicting them, or considering if the methods being used are capable of achieving the new goals. *Id.*

[108] "Strategic drift" is an issue of methods, where the party, "over time, moves away from an effective [method of pursuing their goal] toward a less desirable one, as a result of a series of small steps." ROGER COURTNEY, STRATEGIC MANAGEMENT FOR VOLUNTARY NONPROFIT ORGANIZATIONS 101 (2002).

build a level of situational awareness in the attorney that allows him to foresee what might distract others and to understand how to minimize the damage or exploit the distractions, should they arise. Building this situational awareness is discussed in subparagraph (b), *infra*, and then expanded upon throughout Chapter 4, part (B) (with regard to Effects and Aims). Adversaries may also initiate distractions in an attempt to shape our conduct, a topic that will be discussed in Chapter 5, part (C), *infra*. Right now we will discuss distractions caused by bounded rationality.

a. *Bounded Rationality in Other Parties*

The term "bounded rationality" captures the fact that human thinking is limited by:

- mental ability,
- the information a person has, and
- the time he has available (or is willing to commit) to process it.[109]

Information asymmetry creates opportunities to exploit bounded rationality offensively. For example, during the trial discussed in the case study, the government questioned Defendant as to why he attempted to return Mrs. V's potato chips so late at night, knowing she was probably asleep at the time. Defendant explained that if she was asleep, he planned to leave her potato chips on her front steps. He could leave the food outside, he said, because there were no loose dogs or wildlife in the neighborhood that would eat it.

Government counsel later cross-examined Defendant's wife who had not heard her husband's testimony but was testifying in aggressive support of him, trying to undermine every theory the prosecutor offered. The prosecutor framed his question just as Defendant had responded, "Your husband did not have to enter the house, did he? He could have left the food outside on the steps, right?" As expected, Defendant's wife contradicted him (and, unwittingly, her husband), asserting that there were all kinds of animals loose in the neighborhood. She had even seen a coyote on the street that morning.

---

[109] Reinhard Selten , *What Is Bounded Rationality*, in BOUNDED RATIONALITY: THE ADAPTIVE TOOLBOX 13–14 (Gerd Gigarenzer & Reinhard Selten eds. 2002).

Her act was rational, but only boundedly so—with more information, she would presumably have testified differently. By understanding her purpose (supporting her husband) and her source of utility (contradicting / undermining the prosecution), government counsel enabled her to create unexpected friction for the defense by doing what she thought was in their interest.

b. Our Bounded Rationality and Analysis Paralysis

A person's mental limitations, incomplete information, and time restrictions, (their bounded rationality) leave most with the inclination to find the first workable solution (or the best among several solutions, any of which should get the job done), then forge ahead with it rather than delaying action to ponder whether they have achieved the optimal solution. This desire to work with the first "good enough" solution is called "satisficing."[110] Satisficing is bounded rationality put to good use. When a person fails to satisfice, they often lapse into analysis paralysis.

Analysis paralysis is delaying a decision to gather more information or to further examine possibilities despite needing to act quickly. Once we have the essential information, the cost (in time) of gaining more information generally outweighs the value of the improvement that the further information makes to the final decision. As depicted in Figure 7, in most cases we can gather the bulk of the information needed for our decisions quickly, and make a decision of decent quality. Gathering more details and exploring the various nuances of the situation, in general, takes much longer while only improving the decision by small degrees.

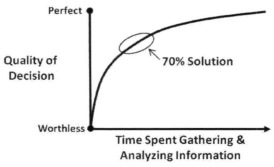

Figure 7: The Seventy-Percent Solution

---

[110] Gary Klein, *The Fiction of Optimization, in id.* at 103.

Satisficing, making a decision based on the bulk of information immediately available, generally achieves a "seventy-percent solution."[111] The decision may not be perfect, but it will get the job done quickly and effectively. General Patton captured this eloquently, stating, "A good plan violently executed now is better than the perfect plan next week."[112]

Satisficing is not all good though.[113] We saw Defendant's wife satisfice only to undercut her husband's testimony. To prevent one's satisficing from being exploited like this, one needs to maximize their situational awareness *before* they are called upon to make the clutch decision. They must spend extra time in analysis before the time becomes precious. This is primarily done through pretrial preparation. As General Patton's contemporary, General Eisenhower, observed, "planning is indispensable."[114] Logically, preparation—analyzing the situation when one is not bound by the need for action and the stress of conflict allows more time to gather and consider information and reduces the chance of succumbing to a cognitive error founded upon bounded rationality.

---

[111] This concept has long been discussed in the Marine Corps, though for discussion in an academic text, *see* Michael Useem, *Decision Making as Leadership Foundation*, *in* HANDBOOK OF LEADERSHIP THEORY AND PRACTICE 514 (Nitin Noria & Rakesh Khurana eds. 2010). The "seventy percent" however is a rounded figure. Studies in a parallel situation, use of information on hand (vice ensuring collection and analysis of all potential information, as with the graph here) show that the speed with which information is processed is based on prior experience in similar situations (as with intuition). Studies show that given a non-life-or-death decision, experienced people generally act on roughly 55% of the information available, while less-experienced individuals consider 65% before acting. Thus experience offers the strategist an advantage in speed of decision making, though at the cost of using assumptions (see the discussion of schema in Chapter 5, part B, below) instead of actual information. *See,* MONISHA PASUPATHI, HOW WE LEARN, lect. 23 (2012)

[112] U.S. MARINE CORPS, MCDP 5: PLANNING 27 (1997) [hereinafter MCDP 5].

[113] Consider also, the availability bias, where the person's most recent experience affects his interpretation of the current situation as well as the likely solution (the "law of the instrument").

[114] Daniel Mogendorff & Hans Strikwerda, *How to Apply the Strategy Map Successfully*, *in* EXECUTING STRATEGY IN TURBULENT TIMES 49 (J. Strikwerda ed. 2007).

Consider the "Monty Hall Problem," which is based on the game show Monty Hall hosted, *Let's Make a Deal*.[115] The problem offers three doors, one of which hides a prize such as a new car. The contestant's goal is to pick the door hiding the prize; he gets one guess, then a "clue," and then an opportunity to switch. Suppose the contestant picks Door 1. The host then assures him that it was a better pick than, say, Door 3, because Door 3 was a loser (this is the "clue"). But there's still Door 2. The host asks the contestant if he would like to switch to Door 2 or if he wants to stay with Door 1. This creates the situation depicted in Figure 8.

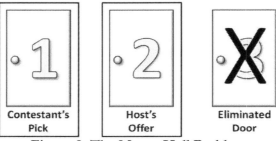

Figure 8: The Monty Hall Problem

Is there an optimal answer? The contestant is choosing between two doors, so he appears to have an even, fifty-fifty chance of choosing correctly. That perception, however, is the result of bounded rationality. We have more information that is not being considered. Specifically, when the contestant picked his door, he had a one-in-three chance. That left the host with two doors and a two-thirds probability of having the prize. True, the host then has to open one of his doors, but that has no impact on the odds. When the prize is behind Door 2, the host opens Door 3. If the prize is behind Door 3, the host opens Door 2.

---

[115] *See, e.g.*, MARILYN VOS SAVANT, THE POWER OF LOGICAL THINKING 5-15 (1996) (The author describes both the problem and the solution offered here. She wrote on this problem in an article prior to writing the book, and—proving the power of the deception at work in the problem—the book includes responses to that article from a number of Ph.D's who insisted this solution is wrong despite its inescapable logic. However, many readers held trials (including computer scientists at the Los Alamos National Laboratory who had a computer run the problem one million times) and "discovered" empirically that switching yields a "win" roughly sixty-six percent of the time—e.g., sixty-six and seven tenths percent of the time at Los Alamos).

The contestant always has a one-in-three chance of picking right initially. The two-in-three chance that the host has the prize is not diminished by him telling us something we already know: that at least one of his doors does not have the prize.[116] What changes when the host opens a door is our *perception*. He leaves us staring at two doors, and bounded rationality (specifically, hasty satisficing) causes us to disregard the third door and everything it means.

In fairness, though, this is only satisficing if the person thinks about it. He might instead have used intuition. Intuition is generally the result of the mind quickly matching key elements of the present situation to a similar situation in the memory, and using this similar memory to offer insight on the present.[117]

Most people have seen so many heads-or-tails, pick-the-left-hand-or-right situations that when first confronting the Monty Hall Problem they might not bother to think—intuition simply tells them that this is just another fifty-fifty scenario. Intuition deceives the person, producing the wrong analogy because he is looking at two doors, disregarding the third.

In the complex situations faced during trial, an attorney's brain may choose a false analogy, misidentifying key elements innocently or through intentional deception by another party. A person will not understand how his initial thoughts misled him unless he thinks thoroughly about the whole scenario. As Eisenhower suggests,[118] planning before the event can vastly improve the quality of an attorney's intuition and satisficing, allowing him to avoid errors and deceit while responding swiftly to unfolding events.

Planning may still require an attorney to play the odds, as the contestant does in the Monty Hall Problem where the best choice (switching) is still wrong one-third of the time. For example, at the trial in the case study, unrelated to the incident alleged by Mrs. V, Defendant also faced sexual

---

[116] It simply clarifies that if he has the prize—which he will two in three times—it is behind the door he did not open.

[117] *See, e.g.*, GARY A. KLEIN, SOURCES OF POWER: HOW PEOPLE MAKE DECISIONS 31 (1998) ("Intuition depends on the use of experience to recognize key patterns that indicate the dynamics of the situation.").

[118] Mogendorff & Strikwerda, *supra* note 113, at 49 (Eisenhower's full quote emphasized the value of the planning process over the end product: "I have always found that plans are useless, but planning is indispensable").

harassment and maltreatment-of-a-subordinate charges regarding his behavior toward a female corporal, Corporal (Cpl) F, who had posted as duty driver one Saturday while Defendant was the senior sergeant on duty. In this incident, a neutral witness, Sergeant (Sgt) "Neutral," could corroborate that Cpl F seemed unusually cold toward Defendant as the day progressed (which generally supported her allegations of harassment). Sergeant Neutral, however, maintained that part of what Cpl F alleged, the most serious part, could not have happened.

Corporal F's most serious allegation was that at one point Defendant followed her into a sleeping area adjoining the duty area, prevented her from immediately leaving, and made some very specific, explicit propositions. Sergeant Neutral, who was in the duty area (though not the sleeping area) at the time, said he would definitely have noticed if Defendant had gone into the sleeping room while Cpl F was inside, and he recalled no such event. He acknowledged that he was watching television but maintained that the shows were not so interesting that he was unaware of his surroundings.

Unfortunately for the prosecutor, Sgt Neutral was a highly effective witness; he spoke intelligently, remained clear and decisive in his statements, and displayed no feelings for or against either Cpl F or Defendant—he seemed wholly unbiased (i.e. "neutral"). He may, in fact have been distracted by the television when Cpl F entered, or when Defendant later followed, or Defendant's conduct may not have been memorable that Saturday, long before Sgt Neutral was being questioned as part of a sexual harassment investigation. Still, he did not waiver in his assertion that Defendant and Cpl F had never been in the sleeping area at the same time. That level of distraction, he maintained, was unfeasible.

Since Sgt Neutral exuded confidence and intelligence while displaying no bias, the jury would likely believe him over either Defendant or Cpl F. If Sgt Neutral successfully discredited the most serious part of Cpl F's allegation, the jury would have to conclude Cpl F was unreliable and would probably acquit Defendant, even for those related matters that Sgt Neutral did not contradict. The prosecutor could spend his credibility battling Sgt Neutral's decisiveness (attempting to cut down a witness the jury was sure to respect), while perhaps also trying to explain to the jury the counter-intuitive-but-proven-fact that people like Sgt Neutral can be stubbornly certain of things that they did not actually see.[119]

---

[119] THOMAS J. GARDNER & TERRY M. ANDERSON, CRIMINAL EVIDENCE: PRINCIPLES AND CASES 271 (7th ed. 2010) ("In Eyewitness identification cases,

Alternatively the prosecutor could simply co-opt the positive elements of Sgt Neutral's testimony (that Cpl F was increasingly cold toward Defendant) and avoid mention of the situation Sgt Neutral would contradict, thus putting Sgt Neutral in a position to support Cpl F rather than undermining her. Doing this, however, would require that the defense counsel cooperate in avoiding the contested portion of the allegation, as well.

Having seen the defense team in action to date, the prosecutor felt the odds favored a tactically oriented (vice a strategically oriented) defense. He felt that if he could make it appear to favor the defense's immediate interests (short-term utility), then the defense would avoid discussing the matters Sgt Neutral would contradict. In playing these odds, the prosecutor called Cpl F to testify before Sgt Neutral, and asked her nothing about being cornered in the sleeping area. As he had predicted, the defense counsel cooperated, deciding to not have Cpl F raise the questionable incident, further attacking their client.[120] The government's analysis and pursuit of the odds had proven effective.

To summarize, in the midst of the conflict one needs to act quickly and effectively, but bounded rationality or the nature of intuition may work against him. These issues may result from not having the relevant information (as happened to Defendant's wife regarding her husband's statement about animals in the neighborhood), or having the necessary information but not using it correctly (as happened to the defense team, overlooking the significance of Mrs. V's back door, despite that information being available). You can minimize the likelihood of either situation, and many other bounded rationality or intuition errors by building your understanding of the situation (to include others' purposes, sources of utility, and possible distractions or pressing goals) through analyzing the situation during planning—planning before the conflict, before the litigator is debating opposing counsel and jousting with witnesses—before the moment when Patton would be justifiably concerned with prompt action.

---

particularly where no corroborating evidence is available, courts are increasingly willing to permit expert testimony about the unreliability of eyewitness identifications.").

[120] The defense decision not to raise the allegations once Sgt Neutral was on the stand will be analyzed more fully in regard to validating potential courses of action. *See infra* Chapter 4, part B.1.

In planning, the attorney may have no better option than to follow the course of action that offers the greatest *probability* of moving him toward his purpose. Understanding the probabilities, too, requires that the attorney thoroughly analyze the situation.[121]

In planning, depth of situational awareness and consideration of others' sources of utility allows the attorney to predict how others will act, and from this he gains insight into how the overall strategic landscape is likely to shift (or "dance") as events unfold. The attorney should especially strive to understand what information others do not have. Lack of information, like the time available and the adversary's analytical abilities—the components of bounded rationality—can be leveraged to shape conduct (as happened to Defendant's wife) just as introducing fleeting goals can distract one from his overarching purpose. However, in the same way that clearly understanding your purpose helps to prevent distraction, clearly understanding your situation can keep you from falling prey to errors of bounded rationality.

Even if minimized, however, friction will still arise. Others will attempt to surprise you and events may take unexpected turns, so the attorney must remain adaptable if he hopes to confront these situations successfully. Trial lawyers have to satisfice in the midst of sparring with witnesses and opposing counsel. Here, too, planning improves the situation. Intuition (one possible foundation for on-the-spot decisions) relies on the attorneys' understanding of the situation. Likewise, the extent to which his rationality is bounded on the spot will be reduced to the extent he is situationally aware. Thus, even impromptu decisions are enhanced by effective pretrial planning. As Eisenhower said, "Planning is indispensible."

D. From Friction to Maneuver

Understanding what creates friction, the attorney should also understand how opponents will attempt to further increase the ubiquitous, naturally occurring friction of the trial environment. Adversaries will create friction with the hope of causing you to start on more and more sub-loops (those Loops beneath the overarching planning Loop in Figure 5, *supra*), leaving you observing and orienting, and re-orienting and re-orienting, with an increasing level of friction so that you become confused, discouraged, indecisive, possibly panicked, and in any event unable to get to the vitally

---

[121] Chapter 4, part B., *infra*, will discuss an effective method of analysis.

important "act" phase of any Loop so that you can respond to unfolding events.[122] In these situations, if you let yourself fall victim to them, you may reach a point where you either ceases acting, mired in indecision; or, consumed by the desire to do something, anything, you might lash out blindly.[123] You may land a lucky blow, but more often your efforts will be ineffectual or even counterproductive. We must better understand this phenomenon so that we do not fall prey to it.

To dominate your OODA Loop like this, an adversary will often try to operate at such a fast pace that you are unable to process the situation and react fast enough, thereby rendering you defenseless.[124] To counter this (and perhaps even to outpace your opponents) you must speed your own pace through the Loop, contracting it, keeping it tight and efficient.[125]

---

[122]   OSINGA *supra* note 15, at 211.

[123]   LIND *supra* note 21, at 6.

[124]   *Cf.* CLAUSEWITZ, *supra* note 66, at 77 (This is Bk 1, Ch1, sec 4 in other translations) ("The worst of all conditions in which a belligerent can find himself is to be utterly defenseless").

[125]   OSINGA *supra* note 15, at 141.

4 ➤ TIGHTENING THE LOOP, MINIMIZING FRICTION

One can tighten his own Loop through speed, planning, or adaptability.[126] Speed, simply moving faster, allows one to act before the situation changes and to preempt others' actions. Planning (prediction and preparation) facilitates speed. When actions are planned, the orientation and decision-making phases of the Loop are completed before the trial, so at trial the attorney's Loop is contracted to simply observing, briefly orienting (to the extent necessary to confirm this is what he expected), then acting. Analyzing potential situations before the trial, invoking pessimism and healthy paranoia, allows one to anticipate likely points of conflict,[127] predict others' responses, and prepare branch plans that address foreseeable contingencies.[128] In the case study, had the defense been prepared with branch plans, they could have immediately reacted to the prosecution's offense.

When preparation fails, we fall back upon adaptability.[129] Effective adaptation grows from clear sight of one's purpose and maintaining

---

[126] *Id.* at 235-39.

[127] *See, e.g.*, Davis-Perritano *supra* note 8, at 16 (analyzing Clausewitzian "decisive points" in the trial context).

[128] *See, e.g.*, BRUCE BUENO DE MESQUITA, THE PREDICTIONEER'S GAME 66-85 (2009).

[129] Linda F. Dennard, *The New Sensibilities of Nonlinear Decision Making: Timing, Praxis, and a Feel for Relationship, in* HANDBOOK OF DECISION MAKING 231-32

freedom of action. A clear purpose serves as a guidepost when considering various options—those options that do not move one closer to his purpose can be immediately discarded, speeding the orientation phase of the OODA Loop. Freedom of action, the ability to pursue alternate, potentially successful courses of action, having left options open and kept resources available,[130] is one byproduct of a properly designed Line of Operations.

The Line of Operations offers an inherently flexible structure for trial strategy.[131] It captures an attorney's plan in graphic form (rather than text) allowing the attorney to observe the interrelationships of the tasks he must complete in a single sweep of the eyes and to integrate those that support each other.[132] With it he can quickly ensure his plan is valid (comprehensively addressing his situation and standing a reasonable probability of success)[133] and that all the tasks are focused, mutually supportive, and appropriately sequenced to achieve his purpose. The level of organization offered by a written schematic may be critical in complex litigation. For simpler cases, a mentally envisaged Line of Operations may be sufficient to allow the attorney to not only survive on a shifting strategic landscape, but to enable him to gain the other advantages of this framework, speeding adaptations, increasing the number of potential opportunities, shaping the landscape, and dominating adversaries.

The Line of Operations is especially supportive of maneuver philosophy, complementing the clear direction of deliberate planning with the flexibility needed in the changing situations attorneys find on the

---

(Goktug Morcol ed. 2007) ("An organization that refuses to adapt will not survive long in a dynamic and competitive environment").

[130] To the extent this is not self-evident, consider that "[a] person can be misled by false information about the resources at his disposal into believing that he is unable to do what he can in fact do; or he may be wrongly informed about the environment which provides and constrains his opportunities." Stanley I. Benn, *A Theory of Freedom*, FREEDOM 327 (Ian Carter, Matthew H. Kramer & Hillel Steiner eds. 2007).

[131] FM 3-24 *supra* note 14 at 5-7 ("These lines can be customized, renamed, changed altogether").

[132] *See id.* at 5-5.

[133] *See infra* Chapter 4, part B.1.

litigation landscape. Finally, the Line of Operation's flexibility extends from its largest to its smallest components.

Consider the Line of Operations from the trial in the case study.[134] The charges at the trial included not only the burglary of Mrs. V's home and the assault upon her, but also the sexual harassment and maltreatment of Cpl F and (at a different time) another female subordinate, and (along with an alleged co-conspirator) an assault upon a female subordinate while deployed to Iraq.[135] With most of the details and nuance removed (so as to not overwhelm the point here), the prosecutor's Line of Operations for Defendant's trial can depicted as seen in Figure 9 (An explanation of the figure follows).

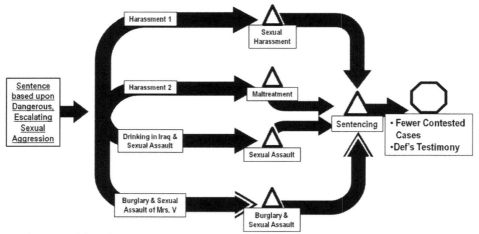

Figure 9: The Skeletal Line of Operations for Government Counsel in the Case Study

The prosecutor's purpose (at the far right, below the octagon) looked beyond the immediate trial. His office was short on staff, a situation that the local military defense bar was exploiting by contesting a greater proportion of their cases with the intent of securing lighter pre-trial agreements as the prosecutors caved to pressure, or (alternatively) acquittals

---

[134] This version of the charges and the intentions of the government counsel is abridged to increase clarity while still drawing upon the actual events.

[135] Because they provide no examples for this case study, the basis for the charges of harassment of the other female and the assault in Iraq will not be discussed beyond their impact upon the charges related to Cpl F and Mrs. V.

as the over-burdened prosecutors made mistakes. The prosecutor wanted to create a disincentive for the defense counsel to contest cases in which they would normally advise their clients to plead guilty in exchange for a reduced sentence. The prosecutor's first criteria of success were achieving a reduction in the percentage of cases his office had to contest. He additionally, wanted to provide Defendant an incentive to testify against his alleged co-conspirator regarding the incident in Iraq (to date, Defendant and the alleged co-conspirator had each refused incentives to testify against the other). The prosecutor's criterion of success here was very specific: Defendant agrees to testify against the alleged co-conspirator. The actual outcome of the case (guilty or not guilty) was not a criterion of success in this instance; the prosecutor had bigger problems. The verdict of the trial would become a prerequisite to success, but it was not a final measure in and of itself.

With criteria of success identified, backward planning begins by determining requirements and variables that make meeting those criteria highly probable.[136] In Figure 9, moving left (backward) from the octagon, we see that the prosecutor intended to achieve these goals through Defendant receiving a stiff sentence for every offense of which he was properly convicted.

Each of the two harassments and two assaults charged appears as a single "Line of Effort" (LOE), a subordinate line within the larger Line of Operations, tracking toward the overall purpose.[137] To achieve a stiff sentence, the LOEs were coordinated for presentation to the jury in a way that would build a picture of a dangerous escalation in Defendant's sexual

---

[136] Backward planning is currently practiced in trial advocacy (though the planning is confined to bounds of the trial). *See, e.g.,* THOMAS A. MAUET, TRIALS: STRATEGY, SKILLS, AND THE NEW POWER OF PERSUASION 19 (2005). "Work backward. Plan your closing argument first, because everything else then follows"). The point of preparing the argument is to identify the key points that must be developed. If one's criteria of success are limited to a specific verdict, then that is exactly what is advocated here. However, the framework herein allows for goals beyond the verdict, and so looks not to argument preparation, but to the reason for this argument preparation: identifying the key factors that must be established for the criteria of success to be met.

[137] U. S. DEP'T OF ARMY, FIELD MANUAL (FM) 3-07, STABILITY OPERATIONS 4-9 (2008) ("[L]ines of effort show how individual actions relate to one [and] other and to achieving the desired end state. . . Commanders . . . synchronize and sequence related actions across multiple lines of effort.").

aggression—the government theme of "growing, dangerous predation" grew from their purpose and the route they chose to meet it. This coordinating measure appears in the box to the left.

Each LOE in Figure 9 displays a triangle, an "aim,"[138] supporting this theme of escalating menace. The first harassment charge (involving Cpl F) would be presented as a basic harassment, a generic orders-violation charge. The second (involving a female subordinate in his unit) would be differentiated as more serious "maltreatment of a subordinate." The assault involving the subordinate female in Iraq (assault being more serious than maltreatment) was then followed by the assault upon Mrs. V in her home (with the invasion of her home presented as making this a more serious allegation). [Had the invasion of Mrs. V's home chronologically preceded the assault in Iraq, the assault in Iraq would have been framed as a more serious offense (he allegedly involved a conspirator and isolated and victimized a subordinate whose well-being he was responsible for). Either event could be depicted as more serious; the prosecutor, of course, chose the framework that supported his theme, which in turn supported his purpose].

The overall picture is one of increasing sexual aggression. This theme, noted on the diagram itself, serves as a guide and a reminder to government counsel to continue to integrate developments accordingly as they present their case.

The first signs of the Line of Operation's resiliency appear here. Each of the LOEs in Figure 9 is disposable. The LOEs create a cumulative effect, but if any one of them fails, the prosecutor might still achieve his purpose through the others.[139] He knows exactly how all the factors come together, so in the event any one of them fails, he has a clear picture—literally, a picture—of what he has lost. If he chooses an alternative action to achieve his aims, he knows specifically what that effort must achieve; if he forsakes the LOE altogether, he can do so knowing the exact cost. By using the Line of Operations construct, an attorney confronted with the

---

[138] "Aim" is a term of art that will be specifically defined in Chapter 4, part B, *infra*.

[139] Though the LOO does designate the LOE regarding the assault upon Mrs. V as the most critical. This LOE bears the double arrow head of a main effort per military symbology. U. S. DEP'T OF ARMY, FIELD MANUAL (FM) 1-02, OPERATIONAL TERMS AND GRAPHICS 7-28 (2004). The concept of main effort, and why this LOE was viewed as more critical, will be discussed shortly.

need to adapt his plan has less opportunity for error, less chance to overlook an effect, miss an opportunity, or succumb to bounded rationality. Further, he will consume less time orienting[140] on changed circumstances because the situational awareness he develops while creating the Line of Operations ahead of time creates a better understanding of the relevant factors and their potential impact. The attorney will move more rapidly through the OODA Loops (both the sub-Loops and his overarching Loop) in compliance with Patton's advice to act swiftly.

Figure 9, however, is merely the skeleton of a plan. Plans should also contain *ways* and *means* (methods and resources) arranged appropriately in time and location.[141] These ways and means will produce *effects* – his impact on the situation, effects entirely within his own control (see the examples in part B, below).[142] Through the effects, the attorney intends to achieve *aims*

---

[140] That is, less time in the orient phase of his OODA Loop.

[141] The core of this is the understanding of strategy as being a combination of ways, means and ends. David Jablonsky, *Why is Strategy Difficult*, *in* ARMY WAR COLLEGE GUIDE TO NATIONAL SECURITY ISSUES VOL 1: THEORY OF WAR AND STRATEGY 3 (J. Boone Bartholomees ed. 3rd ed. 2008) [hereinafter NATIONAL SECURITY]. The elements beyond ways, means and ends are discussed *infra*.

[142] "Effects" are drawn into this construct—in a limited fashion—from "Effects-Based Operations" (EBO), a method of military planning based on considering conflict as a system, and focusing upon the roles of various parts of that system, including the role of the adversary as a system within the larger system of the conflict. *See, e.g.*, GENERAL DAVID DEPTULA, EFFECTS BASED OPERATIONS, 19-20 (2001). The part of EBO drawn into this construct is that part that considers what the individual (attorney) can do within the system (his landscape) to achieve his purpose. The part of EBO expressly barred from the present construct is that which blended action upon a system with the assumption of change in the system (mixing the two distinct concepts this construct calls "effects" (what we can do) and "aims" (what we hope happens as a result of our action)). These problems led to EBO being stricken from use in some areas because of the perception that it created false certainty (unjustified assumptions of affecting desired changes on targeted systems) along with an aversion to risk. *See, e.g.*, John Dickerson, *A Marine General at War*, SLATE (Apr. 22, 2010, 7:10 a.m.), http://www.stage.slate.com/articles/life/risk/2010/04a_marine_general_at_war.3. html. The present construct cures the false sense of certainty by differentiating "effects" from "aims" (as defined *infra*) and noting the need for assessment to determine whether effects have achieved their desired aims. *See, infra* Chapter 4, part B.2. It cures the aversion to action not supported by mathematical certainty by clearly designating the mathematical validation of a plan as a *probability*,

— things the attorney hopes result, but that are not entirely within his control.[143]   We must acknowledge that aims involve factors outside our own control so that we are prepared with built-in redundant effects or branch plans to ensure we achieve those aims).   The aims, in combination, will bring about an *end* (a purpose).[144]   The contents of a Line of Operations as they flow from individual actions and resources to an achieved purpose are depicted in Figure 10a.

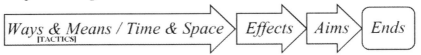

Figure 10a: Contents of a Line of Operations

This seems like a long way to say, "Do things that will create the result you want," but the specific nature of each component makes the trial attorney's Line of Operations a highly effective tool for building plans attuned to the nature of litigation and shaping the course of a trial.   While events will grow from methods and resources (ways and means), the preparation of the Line of Operations grows backward, from the desired final purpose to the present moment, as depicted in Figure 10b.[145]

Figure 10b: Order in which contents are produced during planning.

---

proceeding with the assumption that failing to understand one's likelihood of success leaves him *less* prepared for things to go wrong.

[143] "Aims," as offered here, is derived from the term "*angriffsziel*" or aim point. LIND, *supra* note 21, at 125 ("Angriffsziel . . . the aiming point, that towards which we direct our efforts . . . in order to accomplish our goal."). In the terminology of the present framework "efforts" would be replaced in Lind's phrase with "effects."

[144] "Ends" appear in the standard understanding of strategy. *See, e.g.*, NATIONAL SECURITY, *supra* note 140. The requirements placed upon "ends" as it becomes a term of art in the present construct are discussed *infra*.

[145] Reverse planning avoids the common problem of pursuing promising looking courses of action that never link the attorney to achieving his purpose. It improves the planner's efficiency. *See, e.g.*, GERARDO R UNGSON, YIM-YU WONG, GLOBAL STRATEGIC MANAGEMENT 120 (2008).

It requires some backward jumps and forward nudges (as we saw in the case study Line of Operations in Figure 9) going from achieving a significant sentence in the future back to the present set of preferred charges, then moving forward to characterize those charges in an escalating fashion), but the Line of Operations will largely unfold backward in a smooth fashion from the achieved purpose to the present moment. Since we are working backward from the end, the end is where this discussion of the Line of Operations' components will begin.

A. Ends

If you don't know where you're going, you'll wind up somewhere else.[146]

The "end" has two components, a *purpose* we are trying to achieve and an *end state*, an actual situation embodying the achieved purpose. In the case study, the prosecutor's purpose was twofold: achieving a lower percentage of contested trials and Defendant testifying against his alleged co-conspirator. The end state the prosecutor envisioned to achieve that purpose included Defendant receiving a significant sentence at trial.

A simple statement of the purpose, however, is not enough. The attorney must identify his specific criteria, the ultimate measures of whether he will have succeeded or failed.[147] Sometimes this is relatively straightforward. In the case study, if Defendant agreed to testify against his co-conspirator in that later trial (see below the octagon in Figure 9, supra), the prosecutor will have succeeded as to that one criteria; if not, he will have failed.

Alternatively, the criteria may be more difficult to define, possibly falling on a sliding scale (e.g., the percentage reduction in cases the defense bar chose to contest or, in civil litigation generally, the amount of damages awarded). In these situations, the attorney should still take note of any clear baseline that clarifies what is unacceptable (e.g., any judgment that does not include attorney's fees is a failure). In the case study, though, any reduction

---

[146] LEWIS TIMBERLAKE & MARIETTA REED, BORN TO WIN 38 (1986) (quoting Yogi Berra).

[147] *See, e.g.*, U.S. MARINE CORPS, MARINE AIR GROUND TASK FORCE (MAGTF) STAFF TRAINING PROGRAM (MSTP) PAM. 6-9, ASSESSMENT 6 (2007) [hereinafter MSTP 6-9].

in contested cases would be a success; a larger reduction would simply be a greater success.

For the criteria of success to be accurate (and subsequently for his plan to address the actual issue), the attorney must identify his ultimate purpose.[148] One method for ensuring an attorney has accurately identified this purpose and the accurate criteria is to ask why he is pursuing the goal, then take the answer to that and ask why again and again, repeating the process until he is clearly at the foundation of his motive.[149] For example, in conducting anti-corruption planning in Afghanistan, problems arose framed along the lines of "Judge so-and-so is corrupt." We would then press, "Okay, why do we care?"

"Well, we care because that prevents justice."

"Okay, why do we care about that?"

"Well, injustice decreases the public's perception of the legitimacy of the government."

"Why do we care what the public thinks?"

"Well, we care because our counterinsurgency (COIN) strategy requires popular support for the government, and so the perception of injustice is undermining our COIN strategy."

At this point, we would have our actual purpose and could construct accurate criteria of success (i.e., preventing the corrupt judge from undermining our COIN strategy). Without such examination we would derive misleading criteria, perhaps considering an effort failed if the judge remained in office, even though we might in fact have achieved a successful result, (e.g., if the judge had reformed and was embraced by the community, he could remain in office and the COIN strategy would still be achieved).

Building criteria with this degree of clarity offers three distinct benefits (each of which will be addressed below, and is discussed in greater detail in Appendix B):

---

[148] *See, e.g., id.* at 8.

[149] Aristotle offers the example of an acorn. The purpose of an acorn is not to find nice soil, nor to be warmed in the sun and moistened by spring rains. The acorn's purpose is to be an oak tree. Everything else may be nice, even preferable, but ultimately, if the acorn is in lousy, dry soil in a shady spot, it is still going to try to be a really big tree. That is its purpose, and this purpose will exist regardless of the acorn's situation. The Purpose transcends the situation. *See, e.g.* Stephen Menn, *Aporiai 13-14*, ARISTOTLE'S METAPHYSICS BETA 264-65 (Michael Crubellier and Andre Laks eds. 2009).

- It permits a broader array of possible solutions,
- It reduces the chance of the attorney being distracted by decoys or futile courses of action, and
- It enables him to validate his plan.

Consider how the range of solutions expanded in the anti-corruption example. When the problem is framed as a corrupt judge holding office, the strategy is limiting the possible solution set to impeachment or arrest of the judge, or removing him from office by some other mechanism. As we saw though, the anti-corruption mission could be achieved even if the judge has to remain in the office (which might be the case due to political considerations). In reality, the public's perception of the government's legitimacy could be built by addressing the perception issue, or verifying that there is no perception issue as relates to this judge (in addition to solving the problem, this may allow resources to be distributed to achieve greater across-the-board effects).

Second, clear purpose benefits the attorney during trial when confronted with the need to make a rapid decision or adaptation. The specific criteria of his purpose serve to clearly focus him on what his immediate actions must achieve. Regardless of the fog and the distractions offered by his situation, he can remain on course and not be easily sidetracked. Moreover, the clear statement of criteria will reduce the chance of any one of them being overlooked in arriving at a solution, or of missing an opportunity to ensure his action is taken in a way that provides the greatest benefit to all of his criteria.

Finally, upon completion of initial planning, these criteria are used to determine whether the Line of Operations is valid. Do the proposed actions have a reasonable likelihood of achieving all of the criteria? While nothing can prevent a person from thinking that a jury will agree with even his most outlandish propositions or, more generally, from making ridiculous assumptions, the examination of the causal chain of events in relation to the specifically designated criteria reduces the chance that the attorney will fail to notice that he is relying on such an assumption, or allow him to overlook a necessary requirement or fail to understand the degree of risk he is assuming in following a certain course of action.

The *purpose* should not be confused with a *desired end state*. The purpose is a set of criteria, the end state a situation (albeit a situation in which the criteria are realized). For the Line of Operations in Figure 9, the prosecutor decided that the situation that would realize his criteria was one where

Defendant received a stiff sentence for his crimes [stiff sentence = desired situation; testimony and fewer cases = criteria to be produced through that situation]. The desired end state was no more specific than necessary; it did not dictate which crimes he must be convicted of or how witnesses would testify. It was just a bare minimum reality that would realize his criteria because, as just discussed in relation to purpose, unnecessary restrictions reduce valuable freedom of action while gaining us no benefit.

When more than one end state will achieve the specified criteria, the attorney should generally select the one that is most likely to occur (for example, when rolling three dice, the probability of the sum totaling 3 is .5% because there is only one set of circumstances (rolling three 1's) that can result in a 3; while the probability of the sum totaling 11 is 12.5% because there are six different combinations of numbers that add up to 11—so, metaphorically speaking, the attorney is better off trying to arrange for an 11-type end state than he is for a 3-type end state). Alternatively, if the probabilities are similar in any case, he could angle for the end state that requires the least amount of intervention on his part, exercising economy of force so that he can employ his efforts elsewhere.

Moving backward in time (or to the left on the Line of Operations) from the sentence in Figure 9, we see the end state that is sought in most trials—the jurors' perceptions of the situation. The prosecutor's theme of "dangerous escalation in sexual aggression" supported, but did not wholly embody his desired end state of "sentence severe enough to give Defendant an incentive to testify against his alleged co-conspirator and the defense bar an incentive to reconsider gratuitously contesting cases."

This brings us to the concept of "Main Effort," a subordinate consideration of the end state (which, we saw, is subordinate to the purpose). The main effort is the LOE that will have the greatest impact on achieving the desired outcome. This offers the attorney further focus for his decision-making during planning and, more importantly when pressed to make impromptu decisions during trial. A designated main effort prevents the attorney from having to consider how some factor affects everything by allowing him to first simply consider whether it will substantially help or hurt his main effort. When analyzing the cost related to some potential benefit, he needs to ensure the focus is on the cost and benefit to his main effort. This mental-shortcut allows him to condense his OODA Loop to the essential considerations, speeding orientation and decision-making, allowing him to act with intelligence and focus faster.

In military symbology, the main effort is denoted with a double arrowhead. We see this in Figure 9 on the LOE related to the assault upon Mrs. V. Of all the charges, those related to Mrs. V seemed most likely to yield a sentence of sufficient weight to create the desired incentives for Defendant and the defense bar, so the charges related to Mrs. V became the government's main effort. Everything else he did would serve that end; time, effort, and resources would be apportioned according to that end; and when any opportunity arose he would first consider how it affected his main effort.

Consider the situation with Cpl F and Sgt Neutral—though he was watching television, Sgt Neutral asserted he would definitely have noticed Defendant go into the sleeping area while Cpl F was inside. Understanding that the charges related to Mrs. V were the main effort allowed the prosecutor to quickly understand that Cpl F's allegations about the sleeping area were expendable. They would have less impact than the charges related to Mrs. V even if believed, but more than that, Sgt Neutral's contradiction would likely result in Defendant's acquittal of all the charges related to Cpl F. Any acquittal would be actual proof of prosecutorial fallibility and if the prosecutor could make mistakes (or lack credibility) with regard to one incident this might support a "reasonable doubt" argument by the defense as to any of the charges. Because allowing Sgt Neutral to contradict Cpl F hurt both the main effort and the purpose, the prosecutor did not hesitate in his decision to abandon Cpl F's most serious allegations. He was able to invest the time and effort saved in designing the effects that would shape the course of the trial.

B.   Effects and Aims

Because strategy strives to predict the course of events, it is important to distinguish between what the attorney can absolutely control—the "effects" he can guarantee—and those thing he hopes to make happen—which are referred to herein as "aims." Effects shift the strategic landscape without relying on chance or the cooperation of any other party. If the effect depends upon chance or some other party it is not a certainty, it is an aspiration, a hope—an aim. For example, an attorney can file a motion, question a witness, and present arguments; these are effects because no one can stop him from taking these actions. The outcome of the motion, the answers to the questions, and the ultimate resonance of his argument, however, involve decisions or input from others. These are "aims." One attempts to achieve aims by creating effects that shape other's actions appropriately, or by aligning effects so that our aims are the natural outcome. For example, Figure 11, *infra*, depicts the effects and aims the prosecutor pursued in relation to addressing the defense attack upon Mrs. V's credibility. Because the offense was he-said/she-said, the prosecutor had the aim (far right of Figure 11) of ensuring Mrs. V was perceived as credible. The defense team's pretrial treatment of Mrs. V (in the box on the far left) informed the prosecutor that Mrs. V's assertion that she locked her front door would be the source of an attack. To address this, he intended the effect of introducing his theory about Defendant entering through the back door (see beneath the square) to achieve the aim of having this theory accepted by the jurors as logical. This also made Mrs. V appear sympathetic and credible. He saw that this might achieve the collateral aim of shifting the jury's focus to possible premeditation by Defendant, which would neutralize the defense attack at the same time Mrs. V's reaction enhanced her credibility.

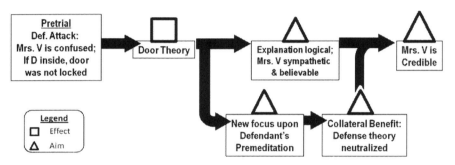

Figure 11: Prosecution Effects and Aims in the Case Study

Differentiating effects from aims reduces the likelihood of unjustified assumptions (a problem mentioned above). Unjustified assumptions can result in stalled efforts or paralysis when events do not occur as predicted,[150] the type of paralysis seen in the defense team when their planned attack upon Mrs. V's credibility suddenly lost its foundation. Had the defense confronted the fact that their attack depended upon Mrs. V remaining baffled about how Defendant entered her home, they might have prepared a contingency plan rather than sitting stunned while their overarching plan turned to a shambles. They could instead have moved directly through the orient phase (where they were stuck) to a pre-planned

---

[150] *See* Dickerson *supra* note 141. quoting General James Mattis, "Some people feel affronted when something they thought to be true doesn't happen . . . You need to be able to be comfortable in uncertainty." "If you recognize war's essential messiness and the enemy's adaptability, you'll reward mavericks, risk-takers, and people who thrive in uncertainty. They'll have the innovative reflexes necessary for a war that changes block by block.").

alternative action.

Differentiating effects from aims also prevents accidentally omitting necessary actions by requiring us to clarify which effects should produce our desired aims. Further, delineating mechanically how one envisions his actions achieving his purpose allows the attorney to avoid taking actions that are attractive but ultimately do not increase the likelihood of achieving his purpose (such as having Cpl F explain how Defendant cornered and harassed her in the sleeping area).

In sum, differentiating effects we control from the aims we hope to bring about offers attorneys the opportunity—across the expanse of the Line of Operation—to evaluate the likelihood of outcomes, to consider alternative means of achieving their aims, and when the probability of achieving them is sufficiently low to build branch plans that circumvent the need for those aims he cannot achieve.[151] We gain further benefit by going beyond simply identifying the variables we control to validate that these planned effects will achieve our desired end state.

1. *Validating Courses of Action*

On a battlefield or in a courtroom, quantifying the likelihood of uncertainties that may hinder or facilitate a particular line of attack will provide an advantage to the party holding such information.[152]

An attorney can "guesstimate" the likelihood of an effect achieving an aim using his experience, and this may be sufficient for many situations. However, the following method makes use of planning time before the trial to methodically break down and assess the potential effectiveness of any individual component of a proposed LOE to provide a higher level of certainty, when this level of certainty is necessary. This process also relies upon experience-based estimations, but by breaking estimations into discrete segments and scrutinizing them closely, it should produce more accurate estimates while at the same time enhancing the attorney's insight

---

[151]   Branches "preserve freedom of action. Branches are contingency plans for changing disposition, orientation, or direction of movement and for accepting or declining battle. Sequels are actions taken after an event or battle and are based on possible outcomes—victory, defeat, or stalemate." U. S. DEP'T OF ARMY, FIELD MANUAL (FM) 100-7, DECISIVE FORCE 3-3 (1995).

[152]   Kris Steckman, *Market-Based Prediction Models as an Aid to Litigation Strategy and Settlement Negotiations*, Vol. II(1) J. of BUS., ENTREPRENEURSHIP & L. 245 (2008).

into the situation.

To understand this process, consider Figure 12, *infra*, as an analogy. One could estimate the width of a whole building by stepping back and looking at its entirety. This might yield an estimate of eighty feet. Alternatively, one could move closer to the building and estimate segments—the distance from the edge of the building to the stair pillar, the width of each pillar and the distance between them, etc. He would then add the estimated segments to produce a different projection for the total (sixty-six feet in Figure 12).

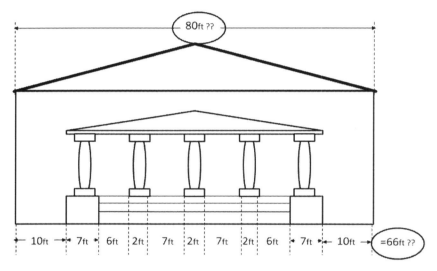

Figure 12: Comprehensive Estimation versus Segmenting

In litigation, the additional scrutiny of a segmented approach provides a better understanding of possible events. It increases the attorney's situational awareness, and when these possibilities become an undesired reality, the prior scrutiny allows him to orient and adapt more effectively (speeding through the OODA Loop) during the trial. But more importantly, scrutiny reveals nuances that affect the immediate outcome. Without understanding nuance, the Monty Hall Problem appeared to be a fifty-fifty choice. Intuition (a "whole-building" type of approach) was unreliable because the important factors lay in the detail. Litigation deals with personalities that, unlike buildings or Monty's doors, are subject to bounded rationality and fleeting or emotional goals. The situations attorneys confront are thus even more deserving of close examination than Monty's doors.

The easiest way to understand the segmenting process offered herein is to walk through an example. Consider the sexual harassment of Cpl F. Sgt Neutral sensed tension between Cpl F and Defendant on the day in question, but did not recall seeing Defendant enter the sleeping area (where the most egregious harassment allegedly occurred). Despite the fact that Sgt Neutral was watching television at the time and had no reason to be suspicious of Defendant, he remained steadfast in insisting he would have known if Cpl F was in the sleeping area and he would certainly have remembered Defendant entering the sleeping area when Cpl F was inside. Sgt Neutral had no identifiable bias toward either party and seemed very intelligent. The jury was apt to like him, to see the unwavering certainty of his statement as compelling, and so to find him very credible.

This posed a problem for the prosecutor. Each of the four LOEs in Figure 9 involved a female accusing Defendant of sexually harassing or sexually assaulting her. With the exception of the third LOE (an alleged assault in Iraq where Defendant was alleged to have acted with a co-conspirator) all of the events were he-said/she-said. Add to this the weight of four women who do not know each other making a similar sort of accusations about the same person and the balance tips favorably toward the government. The weight of the accusations was sure to impact the jurors' perceptions (and their perceptions would determine the sentence[153]). But then there was Sgt Neutral.

Highly credible in his demeanor and with no apparent bias, Sgt Neutral could contradict one significant portion of Cpl F's allegation. This would tarnish the whole of her testimony. This in turn could erode the overall image of the strength of the prosecutor's case, and make reasonable doubt seem more reasonable to the jurors—if one accuser was lying, after all, they could all be lying. Sgt Neutral presented a problem that transcended the Cpl F-related charges, possibly affecting the entire conviction. This jeopardized the prosecutor's purpose.

The prosecutor had the option of combating Sgt Neutral to cut away his credibility (the sergeant was watching television, it was a long day, he had no reason to suspect misconduct, etc). This course of action had no wholly positive outcome—the prosecutor would either reduce this witness the jury liked while still sustaining a smear upon Cpl F's testimony, or expend his own credibility with the jury while failing to convince them of

---

[153] In courts martial, the jury determines the sentence. *See, e.g.*, MCM, *supra* note 83, R.C.M. 1005 – 1007.

Sgt Neutral's misperception and false certainty.[154]   Alternatively, the prosecutor could co-opt Sgt Neutral's positive image by skipping the disputed allegations and having Sgt Neutral simply corroborate Cpl F's cold attitude toward Defendant as the day progressed.

If Cpl F never explained what allegedly happened in the sleeping area, Sgt Neutral's statement that Defendant did not enter the sleeping area would mean nothing to the jury; the threat he posed would be eliminated. Corporal F could testify about her less-serious allegations only, and then Sgt Neutral would follow, supporting the negative tension between Defendant and Cpl F. Of course, this required that the defense counsel cooperate by not raising the serious issue themselves in order to discredit all of Cpl F's allegations.

In pretrial planning, the prosecutor wanted to validate that his planned effect (not questioning Cpl F about her most serious allegations) would result in his aim (Sgt Neutral not discrediting Cpl F). Figure 13 depicts this portion of the LOE.

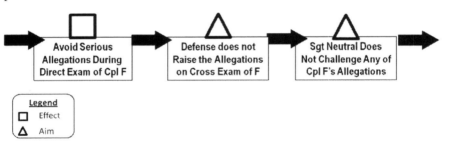

Figure 13: Abstract from the Cpl F Line of Effort

[Note that here, too, we see the value of separating what we control (effects) from those things beyond our control (aims)].

The prosecutor assessed that if the defense counsel were strategically minded,[155] they would consider the situation closely, possibly considering

---

[154] Because Sgt Neutral was unwaivering in insisting the two had not been in the room together, reducing him to uncertainty would be a drawn out confrontation, while not reducing him, but simply arguing he could be mistaken, would be forcing the jury to weigh Sgt Neutral's credibility and charisma against the prosecutor's.

[155]   Game Theory sorts categories of players as "types." *See, e.g.,* SHAUN P. HARGREAVES HEAP & YANIS VAROUFAKIS, GAME THEORY: A CRITICAL INTRODUCTION 77 (1995); James D. Miller & Debbie Felton, *Using Greek Mythology to Teach Game Theory,* AMERICAN ECONOMIST, FINDARTICLES.COM (2002).

this issue ahead of time as he was. If they were tactically oriented (using a standard amount of forethought but mostly confronting issues beyond their plan of action only as the need arose) the prosecutor expected they would not consider the impact of the government's failure to raise the serious allegations until it occurred at trial.

Figure 14, *infra*, quantifies the degree to which the prosecutor expected the defense to value certain events.[156] Similar diagrams are already used in litigation.[157] The numbers—utility values—are a clarification of the prosecutor's "I think he'd prefer this over that" type of evaluation, but the inclusion of utility values allows preferences to be graded along a single scale. The scale is applied consistently across this situation to score valuations *relative to each other*.[158]

The values are the prosecution's estimations of the amount of utility each possibility offers the defense. Outcomes with more utility are preferred over outcomes with less. For example, the first estimate the prosecutor had to make was how the defense would feel about raising the allegations against their client themselves. He opined that they would

---

http://findarticles.com/p/articles/mi_qa5461/is_2_46/ai_n28963541/?tag=content;col1 (draws effective and entertaining examples of tests for determining game theory "types" from Greek mythology); DIXIT & NALEBUFF *supra* note 23155, at 708 (Kindle Loc.) (in discussing Charlie Brown's situation when deciding whether to try kicking the football Lucy is holding, he must consider whether she is the type that prefers to let him kick or the type that prefers to see him fall flat on his back). In the example with Sgt Neutral, the defense is either the type to maximize short term benefits (tactical) or the type to maximize long term benefit (strategic).

[156] This is an extensive form game as used in and validated by game theory. *See, e.g.,* ANDRES PEREA, RATIONALITY IN EXTENSIVE FORM GAMES 6 (2001) (extensive form games are: "noncooperative games for which the decision making may be represented by a rooted tree with a finite number of nodes and edges").

[157] *See* STECKMAN *supra* note 15251, at 246, 252 (discussing the use of "decision-tree analysis" to "predict litigation uncertainties").

[158] The concept of utility values is drawn from Utility Theory. The metric of measurement is "utils," a metric which varies from person to person and from situation to situation, producing a comparative measurement of the pleasure or benefit gained through a certain course of action. *See, e.g.,* ACHILLES C. COSTALES, et. al., ECONOMICS: PRINCIPLES AND APPLICATIONS 48 (2000) (utils are, "a number representing the amount or degree of utility associated with [receipt of a good or service]").

dislike this. Since the value of that dislike only matters in relation to the other values, and he has projected no other values yet, he can assign this first measure any number he wants. He can assign this dislike a value of, say, negative forty (-40), as long as he assigns the other values accurately relative to this -40. So, if the defense dislikes introducing allegations against their client at -40, then neutralizing those same allegations should be worth +40, zeroing out the negative effect. The values are accurate relative to each other.

In the government's estimation, the defense would like discrediting the rest of Cpl F's allegations twice as much as neutralizing the ones they introduced, so he can assign discrediting the entirety of Cpl F's testimony a +80 (the value of liking something twice as much as +40). Thus, while the numbers do not fall on a scale within the system of English weights and measures or the metric system, they remain accurate valuations *relative to each other*.

In addition to values, there are percentages denoting probability. The percentages account for how courses of action with more certainty are preferred over outcomes with less (e.g., a raffle ticket offering a chance to win a new sports car next week has less value than an old-but-reliable sedan we can drive today). These probabilities, like the utility values, are estimated by the attorney.

The effectiveness of math based upon estimates rather than concrete measurements depends, of course, on the accuracy of the estimates. The accuracy of the values will depend on the ability of the attorney to assess such value, which in turn will depend on his experience with such matters and the information he has available to make the assessments. These are the same qualities an attorney relies upon in making an estimate of the whole problem, so to whatever degree his estimates are currently accurate, they should be more so when he segments his approach, scrutinizing each of his underlying assumptions (and, of course, he gains the added benefit of speeding his OODA Loop by being more familiar with the situation).

For the validation of the effect and aims in Figure 13, if the prosecutor omits Cpl F's serious allegations from his direct examination, then the defense will have to decide whether to elicit the allegations themselves in order to discredit all of Cpl F's testimony. We have covered the defense's loss and return of forty utility points by introducing and then neutralizing the more serious allegations, and the projection that the defense would value discrediting the rest of Cpl F's allegations twice as much as neutralizing the allegations they raised, adding an additional eighty (+80) utility points. We have not yet discussed that the defense might further use the fact that the prosecutor hid the discreditable allegation to reduce him in the jurors' estimation, a result the defense might value at +30 points on the same scale (a bit less than half of the utility they would gain by discrediting Cpl F's testimony—note again that all the values are being kept consistent relative to each other). The reader may find it easier to understand the rest of the explanation by following these numbers as they appear on Figure 14, *infra*.

If the defense chose not to introduce the more serious allegations (not losing or gaining the forty points at all), they would be maintaining the status quo, which has a zero (0) value—they gain no extra benefit by leaving things as they are.[159] This zero value for maintaining the status quo appears along both of the main branches of Figure 14.

Returning to the branch on the "strategic" arm, if the defense does take action, they have no guarantee the jury will find Cpl F to be wholly discredited. The values here need to be adjusted by their likelihood of occurring. If a person has a 50% chance of winning $100, that has a value today of $50.[160] So, when a strategically minded defense counsel thinks he has a 25% chance of discrediting all of Cpl F's testimony (valued at +80), that 25% chance has a value right now of +20.

We can branch the whole scenario out, following the options of strategic and tactical defense counsel, in a decision tree like Figure 14. This figure is most easily understood by starting at the left and following the defense teams' options (an explanation of the numbers derived follows the diagram).

[Note: if you were wondering where game theory might fit into the planning of strategy, you see its major role here. If the brief description of this very complicated tool here is insufficient, consider an introductory book on game theory, or the DVD set *Games People Play* offered by The Teaching Company, which covers game trees like Figure 14 along with a variety of tools and applications associated with them].

---

[159] The defense does not "gain" by not intentionally making their own case worse. Avoiding the serious allegations here maintains the status quo, creating no gain or loss from the present situation.

[160] This is the "expected value." *See, e.g.,* PETER V. O'NEIL, ADVANCED ENGINEERING MATHEMATICS 1139 (2007) ("[W]e obtain the expected value of an experiment by multiplying the probability of each outcome by the value of that outcome.").

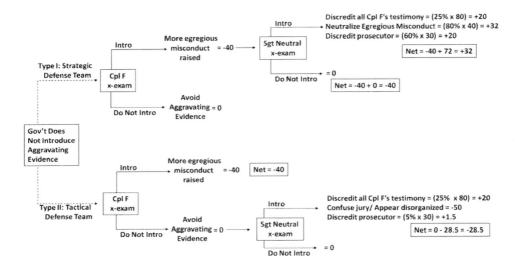

Figure 14: Decision Tree for Validating Defense Response to Government Omission of the Serious Allegations

It would not be helpful to incorporate this decision tree into the Line of Operations. The decision tree tracks every possibility while the Lines of Operation track only the expected course of events and (when they arise) adaptations. The Line of Operations is intended to depict the minimal amount of information necessary to allow the attorney to understand how he desires/expects events to unfold. The type of validation in Figure 14, like the scratch paper from one's math homework, is not attached to the final Line of Operations as it is simply a background justification for the Line of Operations.

Returning to our problem, if the defense counsel were the strategic type (the top branch in Figure 14), he would increase the value of his outcome (+32 by the prosecutor's estimation) by introducing the allegations during the cross-examination of Cpl F, and then attempting to discredit it upon the cross-exam of Sgt Neutral.[161] Given the possibilities, a *strategic* defense counsel would reveal the incident if the prosecutor failed to, and gain substantially by it.

---

[161] To flesh out the rest of the branch, introducing damaging testimony through Cpl F then not discrediting it would, of course, yield only the negative result (-40). Not introducing it at all would, again, result in neither gain nor loss.

The result is the exact opposite for a tactical defense counsel. Here, upon realizing the government failed to mention the serious allegation during his direct, the defense counsel will know that if he raises it, he stands to lose value (-40 by the prosecutor's estimation). The tactical advantages of not introducing serious allegations against one's client are self-evident. Since he is a tactical type, his consideration then stops and the branch terminates at the possibility of "-40."

Once Sgt Neutral is on the stand, the tactical defense counsel will realize the strategic impact of having not asked Cpl F about her allegations: he is now missing out on the chance to discredit her. Of course, the jury will have no idea what Sgt Neutral is talking about as he discredits her, since all Sgt Neutral can testify to is that he did not see Defendant follow her into the room. He cannot offer context as to what allegedly happened there.[162] The resulting confusion would greatly reduce the defense teams' chance of discrediting all (or possibly any) of Cpl F's testimony, and of discrediting the prosecutor in the process (after all, the defense had "forgotten" to ask Cpl F about it, too, so how can they fault the prosecutor for not mentioning it). It would cost the defense in terms of the jury disliking being confused, and the defense appearing disorganized. For the tactical defense counsel, introducing the sleeping-area allegations during Sgt Neutral's testimony results in a net loss.

So, through validating whether the effect will produce the aims in Figure 13, the prosecutor can take the effect as valid/probable by his estimation if the defense is tactical, but invalid/unlikely if the defense is strategic. Further, he has gained an excellent understanding of how events might play out and so will not be wholly surprised, regardless of which path the defense follows at trial.

In the actual trial, the prosecutor opined that the defense was tactically oriented and so he omitted the serious allegations. As predicted, the defense avoided them as well.[163] Cpl F's less serious allegations, in the end,

---

[162] The defense could try to wedge some context in through a hypothetical or a "were you aware" question, but the prosecutor was prepared to turn such an approach to the further disadvantage of the defense. Rather than running down each of these rabbit holes and cluttering the central example with "what ifs," the discussion will focus on the core of the analysis.

[163] In the trial, defense counsel asked Cpl F nothing about the more serious allegation. When Sgt Neutral took the stand, he asked one question to the effect of, "Defendant never went in the sleeping area, did he?" But then withdrew the question and did not raise the issue again.

were circumstantially supported by Sgt Neutral's observations about her demeanor, while the mass of the related accusations by all the women accusing Defendant remained uncontested by anyone but the defendant (and his alleged co-conspirator in regard to the alleged assault in Iraq).

Upon validating an effect, if the probability is low, or even if the probability is high, but the effects of failure will have a significant impact, the attorney should prepare a branch plan so he knows exactly what he will do if events do not favor him. This will be discussed further in the next section on assessing LOEs during execution.

Figure 14 validated that an effect would achieve an aim, however the attorney also needs to step back and validate the overall Line of Operations. No further decision trees are required; the Line of Operations has laid itself out to enable the attorney to apply logic to a visually-comprehensible diagram of his plan so that he can:

- ensure his effects do not conflict with each other,

- identify opportunities to leverage effects off of each other, (the way the premeditation introduced through the theory about the back door served as aggravation in support of the government's sentencing argument), and

- ensure that the Line of Operations, as a whole, addresses every aim required to achieve his purpose's overall criteria of success.

2. Assessing LOEs During Execution

Valid LOEs must be executed with flexibility[164] and a constant focus on achieving their purpose—if they fail to achieve their purpose, the effort is wasted and the larger Line of Operations may fail. And the attorney must be mentally prepared for any LOE to fail—a "valid" LOE denotes only that the outcome is probable, and the odds do not always work in one's favor

---

[164] Flexibility is required due to the dancing landscape and the unpredictability of other parties. *See supra* Chapter 3. The term for a "flexible" plan in business is "dynamic." Whereas a static strategy is formulated and pushed forward, as is, until it either succeeds or fails, a dynamic strategy is formulated, but then intelligently adapted to account for new information, newly acquired skills and resources, or other developments in the situation. *See, e.g.*, FRANCES FORTUIN, STRATEGIC ALIGNMENT OF INNOVATION TO BUSINESSES 18-19, 24 (2007).

(e.g. switching doors in the Monty Hall Problem has a 33% chance of leaving the contestant with the losing door). When an LOE fails, the attorney does not want to stall in the *what-can-I-do-about-it* part of the orientation phase of his OODA Loop. Fortunately, having differentiated his effects from his aims will help to tighten his Loop here, too.

The process of evaluating LOEs during execution to determine success or failure is called assessment.[165] Assessment asks two questions:[166]

- Are we doing things right (did we complete our effect)? and
- Are we doing the right things (did completing our effects achieve the aim)?

The first question examines whether we actually achieved the effect we wanted. For example, did we make the right motion or argument? Did we manage to have Cpl F not testify about her most serious allegations? If the answer to an effect like making a motion or asking a question is no, we might get back on track by simply trying the effect again, but doing it right (e.g., ask the question a different way so the witness produces the necessary information).[167] If one fails in an effect such as having Cpl F omit an allegation then, since one cannot (as the law professors say) un-ring a bell, a branch plan will need to be put into effect to achieve the desired outcome through some different effects.

The second question asks, having completed our effects, did we achieve their aim.[168] For example, having had Cpl F not testify about her more serious allegation, did the prosecutor succeed in having her remaining allegations go forward uncontradicted by Sgt Neutral? The "are we doing the right things" question is important because it prevents us from simply repeating the same effect, hoping for a different result (from objecting, then when the objection is overruled, "strenuously objecting"[169]). If one

---

[165] *See, e.g.,* MSTP 6-9 *supra* note 1476, at 1.

[166] *See, e.g., id.* at 11.

[167] *See, e.g., id.*

[168] *See, e.g., id.*

[169] *See* A FEW GOOD MEN (Columbia Pictures 1992) (A defense counsel is berated for renewing an objection, offering no new points for consideration but simply clarifying that she "strenuously" objected).

properly completes an action, producing the intended effect he controls but not achieving his aim (which others have impact upon), he needs to create a different effect to bring about that aim.

3. Summary: Effects, Aims, Validation and Assessment

In pre-trial planning we have the opportunity to differentiate between those effects we control and those aims we hope result, but which other parties can still affect. Carefully validating that one's planned effects are likely to achieve his aims offers an attorney a measurable degree of confidence in his plan, and also provides insight into where a plan may fail. This, in turn creates the opportunity to prepare branch plans ahead of time, or at least to have sufficient familiarity with the situation so that producing a new, properly focused LOE will not unduly interfere with the attorney's forward momentum. Asking the proper questions when we fail to achieve an aim (assessment) tells the attorney whether he can simply retry an effect or whether he must develop new one or embark upon a branch plan (prepared or impromptu).

C. Ways and Means

Ways are tactics, alone or in combination, and as stated at the outset, the existing array of tactics is thoroughly explored in trial advocacy texts.[170] Means are resources. Resources are not confined to the obvious tangibles: finances, computers and legal pads, or even to evidence, witnesses and visual aids. Resources also include an attorney's tactical and technical proficiency,[171] and his determination.[172]

---

[170] See generally LUBET, supra note 3; GITCHEL & O'BRIEN supra note 7.

[171] This is the set of tactics the attorney knows, to include the uses of rules of evidence and procedure. It is not enough, however, to know of a tactic; he must also be able to execute it. Technical proficiency also includes one's skill at argument and persuasion, oratory, narrative, and logic. See, e.g., LUBET, supra note 3, at 32-42.

[172] Determination and self-discipline are necessary to stay focused and adaptive during the case, never giving up, always looking for another way to shift the channel to achieve your purpose. Discipline and determination are also needed for the longer process of preparing a case and, more importantly, preparing oneself—learning tactics and procedure, and practicing oratory and the construction of persuasive narratives and arguments.

Technical proficiency regards the attorney's personal tactical toolkit, the tactics he can reliably execute without stumbling. As shown in Figure 10, supra, the entire line of operations has a foundation of tactics (the combination of "ways" and "means"). Tactics must be able to achieve their effects if the attorney is to bring about his aims and realize his purpose. Tactics are at the root of every strategy, and as the mock trial team's situation demonstrated (where they had a superior argument but could not support it through cross-examination and content delivery), a strategy founded upon tactics that the attorney cannot execute is of little value. Attorneys must spend sufficient time in the trial advocacy books, evidentiary manuals, and the procedural code developing their tactical tool kit if they hope to successfully execute strategy. The more time they spend developing the tactical toolkit, the more strategic options they will have and the more adaptable they will be, ultimately making them more strategically successful.

As resources, tactics are not expendable in the traditional sense; doing something once does not prevent the attorney from doing it again. However, when an attorney reveals a unique method from his personal toolkit he is, in a sense, expending – reusing it risks making him predictable. While an unexploited advantage has no value, the attorney must balance use of that advantage with the need to remain unpredictable.[173] In this way, an attorney will "expend" technical skills as a trial progresses, or over the span of his relationship with opposing counsel.

The personal resources of resiliency and determination, too, bear special note as the discussion of Lines of Operation comes to a close. Both are critical in any endeavor against thinking, determined opponents because such opponents create the need for the attorney to frequently adapt his plan to unexpected developments.

Fortunately, the Line of Operations is designed for resiliency; it can continue to transform and remain relevant, moving an attorney closer and closer to his objective, so long as the attorney has the determination and resources to continue adapting. For example, when an effect fails, the Line of Operations allows the attorney to simply substitute a different effect that will achieve the aim (as depicted in Figure 15).

---

[173] Obviously, if they foresee but can do nothing about an attorney's plans, his predictable behavior is not a problem.

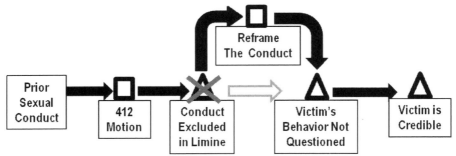

Figure 15: Substitute Effect Achieving the Aim

When an aim cannot be achieved by any means, a different aim or set of aims that complete the LOE can be pursued, as seen in Figure 16.

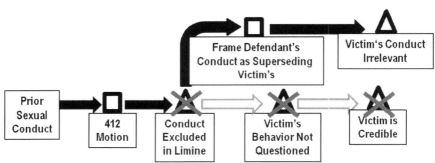

Figure 16: Branch Plan Executed to Pursue Alternate Aim

When an entire LOE fails, if it cannot simply be abandoned (as any of the LOEs in Figure 9 other than the Main Effort could easily be), an alternative LOE that will achieve the purpose can be substituted.

If the desired end state becomes impossible to achieve, another end state that achieves the criteria of success can be adopted. And finally, if a purpose cannot be achieved with any LOE—if there is no way to meet the criteria of success—then having the clearly-defined criteria allows the attorney to rapidly identify where his goals must be scaled back, and thereby allows him to assess whether those criteria he can still achieve justify continuing the litigation.[174]

The strong situational awareness created by generating a Line of

---

[174] In short, he has the information needed to perform an intelligent cost-benefit analysis. *See, e.g.,* TEVFIK F. NAS, COST-BENEFIT ANALYSIS 1-2 (1996).

Operations, and the inherently flexible nature of these plans, allows the attorney to avoid problems from the outset and for those that do occur, allows him to adapt with minimal disruption of his efforts. Of course, the attorney must also be aware the opponents will try to interfere with or shape his actions.

5 ➤ ADVERSARIES' ACTIONS

Clausewitz was concerned with trying to overcome or reduce friction/uncertainty and failed to address the idea of magnifying [an] adversary's friction/uncertainty[175]

This section discusses three ways to affect an adversary's OODA Loop:

- Disruption: Creating new issues so that before completing any single Loop the opponent is thrust back to the observe phase of the same Loop or forced to start a new one so that, in either case, he does not reach the act phase of his current Loop. This includes the extreme of disruption, overload, where the attorney's Loops are so overwhelmed that they cease to function.

- Expansion: Making any individual phase of the adversary's Loop (observation, orientation, decision or action) longer or unproductive.

- Shaping: Affecting the situation or the other party's decision-making so that the actions they take either do not affect, or will actually improve, the attorney's situation.

With all of these methods, the goal is to deny the adversary an opportunity to take effective action. Opponents may pursue your total

---

[175] OSINGA *supra* note 155, at 146 (describing how John Boyd turned friction from something to be defended against into a force to be harnessed offensively).

collapse (as maneuver doctrine advocates),[176] but they rarely require your total functional collapse to gain the advantage needed to achieve their purpose.

The most obvious limits to these offensive uses of maneuver are jurisdictional cannons of ethics. You are responsible for knowing the ethical limitations in your jurisdiction, so you should know when your opponents (and you, should you take this on the offensive) have crossed the line. If they cross the line, you can bring it to the attention of the judge or the bar, but since they may take no action or may not act for a lengthy period, you must also be prepared to continue contesting the trial. To do this you must understand what he's trying to do to you.

A. Disruption

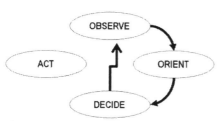

Disruption prevents the opponent from taking action by causing him to stop what he is doing to attend to a new issue. In the case study, we saw the prosecutor disrupt the defense counsels' he-said/she-said theory of the case by focusing the jurors on Defendant's entry into the home. The suggested manner of entry created a new issue of premeditation, and demanded the defense confront problems they were not prepared to confront.

The University of Virginia mock trial team[177] attempted to pre-empt a very solid civil rights, equal-access complaint similarly, by establishing on the merits that the plaintiff was a different party from the person who had initiated the action, and so per the terms of the statute in question, the plaintiff lacked standing. If accepted, this would render arguments on the merits of the underlying claim irrelevant. Unfortunately, while the opposition acknowledged not anticipating the argument, the UVA first-year students had not yet developed the tactical skill needed to corner and drive home points against witnesses played by experienced second and third year students from the opposing team. This rendered the strategy moot.

---

[176] *Id. See also* LIND, *supra* note 21, at 7.

[177] This is the same team referenced *supra* Chapter 1, part A.

In addition to pre-empting the adversary's expectations, an attorney can disrupt his opponent's OODA Loop through task-overload. Some people are highly capable multi-taskers. Humans, however, are only capable of actually *focusing* on one task at a time (to borrow an example, if you think you are good at multitasking, try multiplying seventeen by twenty-four while making a left-hand turn at a busy intersection).[178] Being good at multi-tasking means that the person is able to switch between loops, resuming at about the place he last left off. No one is capable of paying conscious attention to different issues within a single moment, and so contending with numerous issues (multiple sub-Loops, in Figure 5, *supra*) tends to create a backlog, which decreases the chance that the individual will complete any of them, reduces the quality of his analysis (orientation) and decision-making, and can distract him from seeing how any individual issue affects the other sub-Loops or his overarching plan (the big Loop). The additional demands on the attorney consume time and draw his full attention from the action that continues to unfold in the courtroom. When a significant fact or a new issue arises before the attorney re-engages his attention, he is likely to miss it.[179]

Disruption should be used strategically, that is, with an eye to the whole picture.[180] A default attitude for some practitioners is to try to prevent the opponent from achieving anything he appears to want, and to pursue any course of action that might hurt him. We saw this short-sighted approach hurt the defense when they let Cpl F off the stand without discussing her

---

[178] *See, e.g.*, DANIEL KAHNEMAN, THINKING FAST AND SLOW 23 (2011). When people do try to accomplish two tasks that require focus simultaneously, the tasks are vulnerable to failure. *See, e.g.*, LOUKIA D. LOUKOPOULOS et. al., THE MULTITASKING MYTH xiii—xiv (2009).

[179] *See infra* Appendix A.II. (Referenced Comments, No. 1) (once opposing counsel had fixated on his original argument during a motion hearing, the survey respondent switched arguments, using his original argument as a straw man. The judge followed the new argument, but opposing counsel, involved in formulating a response to the original argument failed to address the new argument. The respondent's comment references a similar real-world example from the training presentation, but where the straw man was set up to intentionally distract opposing counsel while retaining the attention of the jury).

[180] Actions that do not serve the purpose are wasteful. *C.f.* FM 3-90, *supra* note 188, at 8-16 ("The commander uses economy of force measures in areas that do not involve his decisive operation to mass the effects of his forces in the area where a decision is sought").

most serious allegations, preventing them from using Sgt Neutral to discredit her.

With disruption, it may be tempting to introduce problems for the adversary with the hope that they will pile up, however, if an attorney is not ready to exploit his distractions or if he lacks the volume to prevent the adversary from multi-tasking through the Loops at his own pace, he may simply be confusing the jury or expending his credibility to no gain.[181] Disruption is most effective when the attorney is poised to exploit it,[182] as the prosecutor in the case study did by disrupting the defense just when they needed to cross-examine Mrs. V, the most critical witness in the government's case.

B. Expansion

One might expand a party's OODA Loop by targeting any or every phase. At the observation phase, she can capitalize on fog and information imbalances. By denying or concealing relevant information (the person's potential "observations"), the party has insufficient information with which to make sound predictions and decisions. Information can also, of course, be concealed in a larger mass of information[183] or slipped past you during some other distraction[184] (as when she introduces a straw man argument to gain your attention, then switches arguments, unnoticed by you but

---

[181] *C.f. id.*

[182] *Cf.* ROBERT A. PAPE, BOMBING TO WIN 316 (1996) ("[S]hort disruptions do not matter unless other instruments are poised to exploit them immediately"). Consider law enforcement or military entry of a hostile room. The entry team does not wait for the dust to settle after the battering ram hits the door or the grenade explodes. The initial impact is followed by the entire team pressing into the room as quickly and noisily as possible, compounding the initial shock to those in the room with more confusion they must orient upon, holding their OODA Loops in the observe and orient phase, making intelligent action difficult if not impossible. In litigation, the attorney must similarly follow his disruptions with more activity that increases the advantage of his position or makes it difficult for the opponent to orient upon the situation the attorney is creating (as was demonstrated in the opening case study).

[183] *See supra* Chapter 3, part B.

[184] The defense against such distractions, should anyone try them against us, is to remain constantly alert.

understood by the jury with their shorter Loops,[185] leaving you discussing the irrelevant straw man).[186]   Information might also be concealed by introducing it in a different context than the one in which she intends to use it.   The case study offered an example of this where the prosecutor foreshadowed his theory of the case by introducing the back door not as a point of entry, but simply as part of a general description of the house; and introduced the fact that Mrs. V did not habitually check her doors and windows not in the context of her return home on the evening of the assault, but rather during a general discussion of her habits.   As noted above, some of the juror's pieced the significance of these facts together, but the individuals who already had built a full picture of Defendant's entry into the home overlooked the prosecutor's real reason for introducing this information.

These attacks upon an adversary's ability to observe are relatively straightforward; attacking another party's orientation phase is more complicated. The orientation phase asks an attorney to answer, *what does this information mean to me* and *what can I do about it*. The process of answering these questions will now be described in depth, but since the core of the material regards perception, and all trial turn on the perception of the finder of fact, the depth of this information will be useful to you in building your case as well as in ensuring your orientation phase is not corrupted.

We all use our past experiences, learning, and values (everything in the

---

[185]   During a trial, the juror's Loops consist largely of observation followed by relatively easy orientation (just placing information into context, a task the attorneys assist them with) and some fast decisions (e.g., whether or not to believe the witness).   Contrast this with the attorneys whose orientation during the trial includes everything the jury must do along with maintaining a mental picture of what the jurors know (the narrower set of facts they have been presented to date) how this picture affects his arguments and overall plan, what testimony or physical evidence being offered is objectionable, and what the effects of objecting will be, and formulating counterarguments and alternative courses of action, and making decisions about which of these to pursue. Thus, the jury has a much shorter Loop than opposing counsel, and so, with fewer distractions, can orient on the transpiring events more quickly.

[186]   While this may seem unusual, the mock trial team supported in relation to this thesis witnessed one opposing team completely fail to acknowledge the existence of their argument, and as referenced above, a member of the focus group reported an instance where he inflicted this on government counsel. *See infra* Appendix A.II. (Referenced Comments No. 1).

bottom bubble of Figure 17, *infra*[187]) to characterize people, objects, and processes.[188] For example, we may think people who wear glasses are smart, and that "going to the store" involves driving a car to a shop, selecting merchandise, and waiting in a line to pay for it. These stereotypes resulting from our experience, learning, and values (second bubble from the bottom) are called schema.[189]

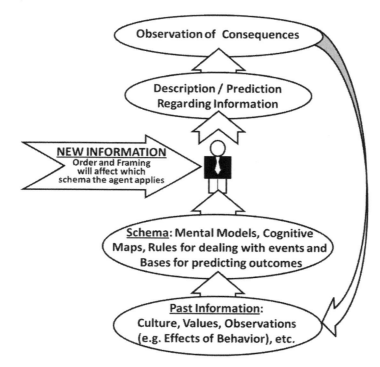

Figure 17: Creation and Use of Schema

---

[187]   Figure is based upon a diagram on the functioning of complex adaptive systems. *See* OSINGA, *supra* note 155, at 99; MURRAY GELL-MANN, THE QUARK AND THE JAGUAR 25 (1994).

[188]   *See* WEITEN, *supra* note 19, at 470 ("Stereotypes and other schemas create biases in person perception that frequently lead to confirmation [as in "confirmation bias"] of people's expectations about others."). *See also* RICHARD C. WAITES, COURTROOM PSYCHOLOGY AND TRIAL ADVOCACY 40-41 (2003) ("First, the juror evaluates the facts, arguments, and technical evidence and constructs a mental summary.").

[189]   WEITEN *supra* note 19, at 470.

When new information comes to us (the arrow from the left) we use a relevant schema to make sense of the information or to predict how it will behave (as seen in the second bubble from the top). Once we observe the thing in action, those observations join the experiences in the bottom bubble. This is how we answer the "what does this mean to me" question of the orientation phase and also informs other aspects of the trial process.

Building a shared awareness with the jury requires establishing a common schema.[190] Before reading ahead, take a moment to consider what schema would the government counsel in the case study want to adopt to invoke the image of a person that harasses subordinates and enters his neighbor's house at night to initiate a liaison with the woman there? What schema might the defense adopt to make the allegations not fit?

In Defendant's trial, the prosecutor's opening statement invoked the image of a person who considered himself desired by women, but who viewed them as objects.[191] The defense offered the counter-image of a family man and concerned neighbor. The set of charges and the early testimony by those alleging Defendant had sexually harassed them fit the government-offered schema more closely, and it is likely that the jurors came to view all of Defendant's actions through that schema.[192] Once a

[190] *See, e.g.*, DANIEL GOLEMAN, VITAL LIES, SIMPLE TRUTHS: THE PSYCHOLOGY OF SELF-DECEPTION 163 (1985). One problem here is projecting our own values, understandings, and assumptions onto others. *Cf.* MICHAEL KUBLIN, INTERNATIONAL NEGOTIATING 14 (1995).

[191] Specifically, due to the demographic of the jury, the government invoked the character "Mike Damone" from *Fast Times at Ridgemont High* to provide jurors a ready-made image into which they could find a context for Defendant's actions. Damone was the fast-talking scalper who put "the vibe" out to every woman he encountered and, because some occasionally responded, he considered himself a desirable ladies man. FAST TIMES AT RIDGEMONT HIGH (Universal Pictures 1982).

[192] When schemas are in conflict, "scheduling" occurs to give one schema primacy. *See, e.g.*, HAROLD E. PASHLER, THE PSYCHOLOGY OF ATTENTION 396-97 (1998); LANCE J. RIPS, THE PSYCHOLOGY OF PROOF: DEDUCTIVE REASONING IN HUMAN THINKING 294-95 (1994).

As an aside, determining which factors affect schema selection can be instrumental in manipulating perception. Sheena Iyengar, a researcher in the decision making field and a professor at the Columbia School of Business, related a story [http://www.ted.com/talks/sheena_iyengar_on_the_art_of_choosing.html] in which she has asked a pair of store clerks to describe the difference between two

schema is adopted, newer, contradictory information rarely causes a person to abandon his first impression. Instead, the existing schema becomes an anchor, a fixed point from which adjustments are made, but from which large deviations are unlikely.[193] Consider again how the police report in the cases study led the defense counsel and the victim to adopt a schema in which the Defendant entered through the front door. Neither witness nor defense counsel questioned that schema while the prosecutor established that Defendant had an opportunity to unlock the back door. It was not until the prosecutor explicitly laid out the likely chain of events that the witness registered shock and the defense team confronted the changed situation.

In addition to affecting others' perceptions, schemas affect our own predictions and the orientation phase of our Loops during trial. If we fail

---

apparently identical shades of pink nail polish, one named "Ballet slippers," the other "A-dorable." The clerks described the difference by saying A-dorable was glamorous, while ballet slippers was elegant. Dr. Iyengar bought both and asked her work colleagues to describe the difference. Several accused her of using identical samples. Of the others, the majority preference was for "A-dorable" when they were not shown the names, and for "Ballet Slippers" when they were.

The emotional state of the receiver of some input can also be a factor. For example, "[r]esearch actually supports the idea that people who are depressed see the world more realistically." THOMAS ARMSTRONG, THE POWER OF NEURODIVERSITY 105 (2010).

[193] *See, e.g.*, Hart, Ledgerwood &. Ianni *supra* note 51.

Also, Abandoning the original anchor is even less likely when a change calls not merely for a different model, but for re-evaluation of the other's core beliefs. Upon hearing, "That cheerleader, Lacey, dealt with her car breaking down" a person might assume 'Lacey called a garage,' or less generously, 'Lacey remembered the car requires an ignition key.' It will likely take direct clarification by the speaker to have the listener understand that 'fix' meant 'Lacey replaced a malfunctioning carburetor and adjusted the timing belt.' It will take further collective action by numerous cheerleaders to get the average person to adjust their mental model of "cheerleaders," even after learning of Lacey's expertise in internal combustion. We have to repeatedly receive contrary information before we will adjust a mental model; one or two exceptions is rarely enough. Instead, if a person does not simply disregard the contrary information or live with cognitive dissonance, as with an anchor point, he will most likely tweak his model just enough to account for whatever contrary information he received.

to adopt the correct schema we will not accurately evaluate our possible courses of action.[194] Pre-trial planning (especially with the depth of scrutiny offered by the segmenting validation system described above), however, helps us to guard against making things conform to inaccurate schema, and offers us time to evaluate data objectively.

One can use the model of observation in Figure 17 to understand his opponent's likely actions, but he can also use it as a means of locating opportunities to create surprise. When satisficing (or succumbing to bounded rationality) people generally adopt the first promising schema they find, and then anchor to it.[195]

This applies to the schema with which attorneys characterize entire cases. Consider the UVA Mock Trial Team experience. The UVA defense team looked beyond the first promising schema (which they expected their opponent's would adopt) and shifted the point of conflict using the previously-mentioned merits-based challenge to plaintiff's standing. The UVA plaintiff team (petitioning the court for structural changes to enable disabled access to a building) undercut a defense based on the most obvious schema, a "historical character of the building" defense, by devising a feasible "more historically appreciative" design of the same facility.[196] Such viable, unexpected alternative schemas (which make surprise possible) may not always be present, but if they exist, they are found most easily by using the pre-trial planning time to understand, and then look beyond, the schema that others are likely to adopt.

Schema might also be leveraged through ambiguity or deception. Ambiguity exists where information has multiple meanings or the situation leaves multiple possibilities open. For example, an adversary asking to negotiate may be stalling for time or genuinely looking for a solution. One cannot be certain which is the case (though he can look to their purpose

---

[194] "Boyd encourages constant repositioning of mental models to adjust and respond more quickly to emerging strategies than an opponent." Major Robert B. Polk, A Critique of Boyd Theory 43 (Dec 15, 1999) (unpublished monograph, U. S. Army School of Advanced Military Studies (SAMS)) (on file at SAMS).

[195] This is an aspect of availability bias. *See, e.g.,* Shelley E. Taylor, *The Availability Bias in Social Perception and Interaction,* in JUDGMENT UNDER UNCERTAINTY, *supra* note 233, at191-92.

[196] The opposing teams in both cases commented that the UVA arguments had caught them unprepared.

and utility[197]). Where ambiguity leaves the other unsure of which schema to apply,[198] deception influences him to apply an inaccurate schema. It can be used to enable surprise, increase your freedom of action (by concealing actions you do not want an adversary to interfere with), and sometimes to cause adversaries to inadvertently assist you.

Consider the ambiguity in the data point that there was no evidence of a break-in at Mrs. V's home. The defense schema framed this as further evidence that Mrs. V had not locked her door (if there was no break-in then she must have left it open); the prosecutor's schema used this to support that Defendant had unlocked the back door while he was getting potato chips from her kitchen. A single data point supported these distinctly different propositions. The government counsel used this ambiguity to allow the defense to highlight the lack of break-in during opening statements, only to co-opt it for his own use, making his argument appear stronger for relying on facts put forth by his adversary.

C. Shaping

Sun Tzu observed, "[T]hose skilled at making the enemy move do so by creating a situation to which he must conform."[199] We saw in the opening case study that shifting the focus to Defendant's entry through the back door preempted (surpassing in perceived importance) the discussion of events in the bedroom, thus affecting the defense's ability to present their planned theory of the case. Motions *in limine*, additionally, attempt to preclude courses of action.

Class action lawsuits are known to compel defendant's to settle, even in cases with a low probability of success, as defendants often prefer to avoid the possibility of paying potentially crippling damages should they lose.[200] With such "class-action blackmail," conduct is shaped by leveraging

---

[197] *See infra* Chapter 3, part C.

[198] This is how one becomes "formless and unfathomable" as advocated by Sun Tzu. *Cf.* OSINGA *supra* note 155, at 38-39.

[199] MARK MCNEILLY, SUN TZU AND THE ART OF MODERN WARFARE 265 (2001) (quoting Sun Tzu).

[200] *See, e.g.*, MARCY HOGAN GREER, A PRACTITIONER'S GUIDE TO CLASS ACTIONS 506 (2010).

rationality. As discussed in Chapter 3 part C, *supra*, rational individuals take the actions that they *expect* will bring them the greatest benefit. This benefit is called "utility."

An attorney can use the amount of utility others expect to receive to steer those people toward or away from particular courses of action.[201] For example, the perceived disadvantage (negative utility) of having an alleged co-conspirator invoke his right to not incriminate himself will often deter the defense from asking him substantive questions.

This, of course presumes efforts to turn the co-conspirator to testify truthfully against the accused have failed, which brings us to the use of utility in the classic Prisoner's Dilemma, a basic of game theory dealing with the manner in which utility shapes two prisoners' decisions about confessing.[202] To illustrate, suppose Ima Suspect and Ben Accused are apprehended by police. The prosecutor has a case that will probably get each a three year sentence, as is. If the police get either to testify against the other, though, the case will be worth ten years. If only one of the two confess, however, that one will be granted immunity in exchange for testifying against the other, so instead of serving ten years, he will serve zero. These possibilities are often depicted in a two-by-two game, as seen in Figure 18 (Ben's result is at the top right of each box, Ima's at the lower left).

Ima \ **Ben**	Remain Silent	Confess
Remain Silent	3 yrs (Ben) / 3 yrs (Ima)	0 yrs (Ben) / 10 yrs (Ima)
Confess	10 yrs (Ben) / 0 yrs (Ima)	5 yrs (Ben) / 5 yrs (Ima)

Figure 18: The Prisoner's Dilemma

[201] Confronting completed action falls outside the scope of the OODA Loop philosophy.

[202] *See, e.g.*, ANATOL RAPOPORT & ALBERT M. CHAMMAH, PRISONER'S DILEMMA 24–25 (1970).

Here utility is measured in *less* prison time. Ima and Ben can consider their options (the utility they will receive through each possible action) and decide independently whether they will confess.[203]

If Ima talks, she might go free. If she does not, she faces ten years if Ben confesses, and three if he does not. Regardless of what Ben does, Ima is better off confessing. The same is true for Ben. So, unless they are willing to do time while the other may walk free, both will confess and do five years when they both would have been better off remaining silent and only serving three.[204] So, perceptions of utility can shape a person's actions, even against his own best interest.

We saw an example of utility shaping the defense counsels' action in the decision tree regarding Cpl F and Sgt Neutral (where, in fact, specific values of utility were estimated and applied to each possible course of action to determine which path the defense was likely to follow). The tactically minded defense counsel saw the advantage of not having Cpl F testify about her more damaging allegations. Had the prosecutor expected the defense to consider the problem strategically, where the utility values were different, he would have had to create different benefits or disincentives to achieve his desired result.

It should come as no surprise that the process for validating a course of action in many respects mirrors the process for shaping events. Validation asks, given the way the attorney expect events to unfold (including the effects he plans to create), will his desired aim result. Shaping asks what steps the attorney can take and what variables he can shift to change the course of events to ensure he achieves his outcome. Validation is a passive examination while shaping inserts new variables or causes the existing ones to be altered to change the likely outcome.

---

[203] It presumes a purely rational approach by Ima and Ben, and yields to no expectation that the other might take pride in not "ratting out" his partner.

[204] The difficult-to-accept outcome of the Prisoner's Dilemma is that perceptions of utility cause both Ima and Ben to act against their best interest (accepting a five year sentence instead of a three year one) and confess, yet this action is completely rational given that if they acted differently, the outcome would be even worse—a ten year sentence for the one who did not confess.

6 ➤ CONCLUSION: A PHILOSOPHY AND A PROCESS FOR LITIGATION STRATEGY

This book set out to demonstrate that the reach and effectiveness of litigation strategy can be vastly enhanced—and that training in litigation strategy can be greatly improved—by augmenting current trial advocacy approaches with a strategic framework drawn from proven concepts and techniques of military science, utility theory, psychology, and systems theory. This article specifically sought to offer a strategic philosophy and a method for ensuring:

1. The attorney's plan is valid:
    o comprehensively addressing his situation, and
    o standing a reasonable probability of success.

2. All tasks are:
    o focused,
    o integrated and mutually supportive, and
    o appropriately sequenced to achieve his purpose.

3. The attorney is capable of:
    o rapid adaptation to changing situations,
    o increasing his number potential opportunities,
    o shaping the situation and his opponent's actions, and
    o responding with a scalable modular system applicable to
        trials of any complexity level.

This system first has the attorney determine his *purpose*, specifying his criteria of success and an *end state* that will achieve that purpose.

Contemplation of the end state that realizes his criteria will clarify the attorney's *aims* at trial, those individual conditions necessary for the end state to become a reality—conditions which are beyond the attorney's complete control, but not beyond his influence. The attorney then decides what *effects* he can create, what influence he can wield, to achieve his aims. He can even validate the likelihood of those effects achieving his aims though a segmented analysis that considers what the parties involved want (what brings them utility) and how likely they are to achieve it.

By working backward from his desired outcome and addressing his requirements, the attorney has ensured his actions are focused and mutually supportive, appropriately sequenced and stand a reasonable probability of success. Because this process resulted in a diagram that is easy to comprehend from start to finish,[205] the attorney can now complete his validation by checking that he has comprehensively addressed the requirements of his criteria of success and he has a clear vision of the actions he must take. From here, he can see where he can combine effects for mutual support, and de-conflict them to ensure he is not working toward one aim by working against another. And at this point, the framework has delivered as promised on the list above under items 1 and 2, along with the second bullet under item 3.

This book also demonstrated that the Line of Operations is more than just a static plan; it is an inherently adaptable product that supports dynamic execution. The desired outcomes of the attorney's effects, the aims, are clearly identified allowing for alternate methods to be pursued by simply adding additional effects or a branch to any of the subordinate LOEs. If necessary, entire LOEs can be substituted for others that achieve the same, already-identified aims or different aims that support the desired end state. Even the end state itself may be discarded, if necessary or practical, for another that achieves the attorney's criteria of success.

Just as the individual LOEs are modular, so is the entire system. Individual concepts, such as utility-based predictions or course of action validation, can be integrated or disregarded as desired. Similarly, as the survey results show[206] and as was described *supra*, the attorney has the option of fully charting out his complex case in an easy-to-scan diagram, or of using the Line of Operations mentally to clarify his strategy for routine,

---

[205] *See supra* Figures 9, 11, 13, 15–16.

[206] *See infra* Appendix A.

uncomplicated trials. Thus, the framework is modular and scalable to meet the attorney's needs and time constraints.

This adaptability is enabled by the Line of Operations, but is directly a product of the underlying philosophy of maneuver. The attorney's understanding of maneuver presses him to act rapidly and effectively so that his opponents are reacting more often than acting. He keeps his OODA Loop tight through having prepared well, and through the speed with which he can pursue the contingencies that he identified while validating his effects and examining his concise Line of Operation.

He understands how OODA Loops are affected by multiple, difficult problems, expanded by slowing orientation and decision-making, or by shaping actions using the concept of utility. In this way, the attorney is rapidly adapting, increasing his opportunities through his greater skill set, and if not controlling the course of events, at least nudging the rudder enough so that he is likely to achieve his purpose. Thus, all of the criteria on the list above are met.

Moreover, we have a philosophy and a process that can be clearly articulated in the training of trial advocates,[207] and which will fully support their further development—the adaptability of this framework supports incorporating other methods that may evolve in the attorneys practice, or that he may learn through the further study of military science, utility theory, psychology, or systems theory.[208] If chance does favor the prepared mind (a premise quoted at the outset of this article), then the framework presented offers a flexible, effective method of gaining chance's favor.

---

[207] Note that while this article demonstrated that tactical ability is a requirement for strategic execution, there is no reason to delay training in strategy until the student is comfortable with his foundation. Strategy and tactics are complementary disciplines, there is no linear progression from one to the next and, logically, there are advantages to learning each in conjunction with the other.

[208] These fields include the subordinate disciplines of game theory, complexity theory and chaos theory.

APPENDIX A ➤ SURVEY RESULTS

I.   Live Presentation Survey Data

The following is the raw data collected from the focus group that attended one of two live presentations. Surveys were distributed prior to the presentation. Respondents submitted them anonymously in a folder outside the room afterward. The participants in the focus groups were volunteers from the 185th Army Judge Advocate Officer's Basic Course and the 39th Criminal Law Advocacy Course at The Judge Advocate General's Legal Center and School.

Respondent:	1	2	3	4	5	6	7	8 [209]
1) In how many contested trials have you taken part in preparing the trial strategy?	0	0	0	0	0	5	10	>200

---

[209] Respondent 8 appeared to have firewalled his responses without considering the questions.

2) To what extent does this material help you better understand competitive interaction in a way that will be useful at trial?	2-Much	3-Some	3-Some	2-Much	3-Some	2-Much	3-Some	2-Much	1-Very Much
3) Do you believe the material presented will be of value to you _outside_ of trial practice?		2-Much	2-Much	1-Very Much	1-Very Much	2-Much	3-Some	2-Much	1-Very Much
4) Is the "foggy, dancing landscape" a useful way for you to think about conflict?			1-Very Much	3-Some	1-Very Much	1-Very Much	3-Some	3-Some	1-Very Much
5) Do you believe the material on how to maximize others' friction will be useful to you?			2-Much	3-Some	1-Very Much	3-Some	3-Some	2-Much	1-Very Much
6) Do you believe the material on how to minimize your own friction will be useful to you?			2-Much	2-Much	1-Very Much	2-Much	2-Much	1-Very Much	1-Very Much
7) Do you expect you physically (or electronically) draw lines of operation for your future contested cases?			Yes	Yes	Mentally	Mentally,	Yes	Mentally	Yes

Question								
8) Do you expect you will specifically differentiate Purpose from End State when planning in the future?	2-Often	3-Sometimes	1-Always	1-Always	3-Sometimes	3-Sometimes	1-Always	1-Always
9) How useful do you believe differentiating Effects from Aims will be for you?	4-Barely	3-Some	1-Very Much	2-Much	3-Some	2-Much	2-Much	1-Very Much
10) How useful do you believe Measures of Performance (measuring your Effects) and Measures of Effectiveness (measuring your achievement of aims) will be for you in trial practice?	2-Much	4-Barely	1-Very Much	3-Some	3-Some	2-Much	2-Much	1-Very Much
11) How much do you believe this material will improve your effectiveness as a trial attorney?	2-Noticeably	3-Slightly	2-Noticeably	1-Vastly	3-Slightly	2-Noticeably	3-Slightly	1-Vastly
12) How Much do you believe this material will improve your efficiency as a trial attorney?	2-Noticeably	4-Barely	3-Slightly	1-Vastly	-1 Worse	2-Noticeably	3-Slightly	1-Vastly

13) Do you believe the OODA-LOO system integrates the various elements of trial (opening, cross-exam, closing and even theme and theory) better than Theme and Theory alone?	Yes	Yes	Yes	Yes	No Opinion on this	Yes	Yes	Yes

II. On-Line Presentation Survey Data

The following is the raw data provided by the survey of the on-line focus group, which included non-voluntary, professionally obligated participants.

1. If you are in the military, of what branch are you a member?		
Army	8	40%
Navy	2	10%
USMC	0	0%
USAF	7	35%
USCG	3	15%
I am not in the DoD/DHS	0	0%
Total	20	100%

2. Please indicate your status.		
Active Duty	20	100%
Reserve or National Guard	0	0%
Not Applicable	0	0%
Total	20	100%

3. In (approximately) how many contested trials (civilian or military) have you taken part in preparing the trial strategy?		
None	0	0%
Less than 10	7	35%
11-20	7	35%
21-50	5	25%
51 or More	1	5%
Total	20	100%

4. How many other trial attorneys do you supervise?		
None	13	65%
1-5	3	15%
6-10	2	10%
11-20	1	5%
More than 20	1	5%
Total	20	100%

5. Is your current billet as Trial Counsel or Supervising Trial Counsel, or as Defense Counsel or Supervising Defense Counsel?

Trial Counsel (Prosecutor)	8	40%
Defense Counsel	9	45%
Neither / Not Applicable	3	15%
Total	20	100%

6. Please mark one answer per question.

Top number is the count of respondents selecting the option. Bottom % is percent of the total respondents selecting the option.	Very Much	Much	Some	Not Much	Not at All	I don't Know
To what extent does this material help you better understand competitive interaction in a way that will be useful at trial?	2	4	9	4	1	0
	10%	20%	45%	20%	5%	0%
Do you believe the material presented will be of value to you outside of trial practice?	3	2	9	6	0	0
	15%	10%	45%	30%	0%	0%
Is the "foggy, dancing landscape" analogy a useful way for you to think about conflict?	4	5	6	4	1	0
	20%	25%	30%	20%	5%	0%
Do you believe the material on how to maximize others' friction will be useful to you during your career as a trial attorney?	4	5	7	3	1	0
	20%	25%	35%	15%	5%	0%
Will the material on how to minimize your own friction will be useful during your career as a trial attorney?	1	6	10	2	1	0
	5%	30%	50%	10%	5%	0%

7. Do you expect you will physically (or electronically) draw lines of operations for your future contested cases?

Yes	3	15%
No	10	50%
I expect I will use this in my mind, but without drawing	7	35%
Total	20	100%

8. Please mark one answer.

Top number is the count of respondents selecting the option. Bottom % is percent of the total respondents selecting the option.	Always	Often	Sometimes	Never	I did not understand the distinction
Do you expect you will specifically differentiate Purpose from End State when planning in the future?	4	7	8	0	1
	20%	35%	40%	0%	5%

9. Please mark one answer per question.

Top number is the count of respondents selecting the option. Bottom % is percent of the total respondents selecting the option.	Very Much	Much	Some	Barely	Not at All	I did not understand the distinction
How useful do you believe differentiating Effects and Aims will be for you when considering strategic action?	0	4	11	3	2	0
	0%	20%	55%	15%	10%	0%
How useful do you believe Measures of Performance (measuring your effects) and Measures of Effectiveness (measuring your achievement of aims) will be for you in trial practice?	1	2	10	4	3	0
	5%	10%	50%	20%	15%	0%

10. Please mark one answer per question.

Top number is the count of respondents selecting the option. Bottom % is percent of the total respondents selecting the option.	Vastly Better	Noticeably Better	Slightly Better	Barely Better	The Same	Worse	I can't imagine
How much do you believe this material will improve your effectiveness as a trial attorney?	0	4	6	3	6	0	1
	0%	20%	30%	15%	30%	0%	5%
How much do you believe this material will improve your efficiency (the time it takes you to build a trial strategy)?	1	2	6	2	8	0	1
	5%	10%	30%	10%	40%	0%	5%

11. Do you believe the OODA-LOO system integrates the various elements of trial (Opening, Cross-exam, Closing, and even Theme and Theory) better than Theme and Theory do alone?

Yes	10	50%
No	6	30%
I have no opinion on this	4	20%
Total	20	100%

Referenced Comments:

1) Without having knowledge of your OODA-LOO model I accidentally used parts of it at a GCM in October. I'd love to say it was my design from the beginning, but it was not. I was lead defense counsel on an Article120 [Rape & Sexual Assault] preparing to argue a 412 motion [Rape Shield]. Written motion was already submitted TC and the Court. The 412 evidence was absolutely necessary for our defense, I did not want to expose my theory of the case so early in the game to TC [Government Attorney] but it was obvious that it was necessary to do so in order to have a fighting chance during the 412. My argument had flaws, which the TC exploited in their written response. Nonetheless, I was confident that I could convince the MJ [Military Judge] and aggressively prepared. From my time as a civilian attorney I've always employed the theory "reread the case file until

you know all of the facts, then read the case file 2 more time until you understand them." I read the case file again, oriented myself to the new understanding I had, made a decision on a new theory, and decided to act. At the Article 39 [motions hearing] I moved forward on my originally theory (LOO) [Line of Operations], arguing just enough for TC to start taking notes, then shifted gears into the new/real theory (my restructured LOO). Amazingly, as I made the transition the MJ made a comment acknowledging the new argument. In rebuttal the TC spent most of their time focusing on the initial theory. The new theory was addressed but not sufficiently. The MJ's response of the 412 was favorable for the defense, did not get everything but got what was important. At trial the TC never readjusted to address the new theory. The accused received a full acquittal. The entire process was accidental, but after watching your training it loosely fits into your model. Knowledge of your model would have made my process a lot more efficient.

2) Much of your briefing I have seen in practice but I have never heard it actually discussed. Much of what you discussed, I had thought of generally in my mind but with you presenting the topic in the easy to understand way that you did, it gives shape to some of the ambiguous ideas that I had floating around in my mind. By far, this briefing was the best trial strategy information that I have received from the military. However, I do think the material you briefed on may be difficult for beginner trial practitioners to grasp because until you have the mechanics of trial practice down, I do not think you can incorporate your ideas effectively. Overall though, great information and briefing.

APPENDIX B ➤ THE ADVANTAGES OF CLARIFYING PURPOSE

[THE FOLLOWING ROUGH CHAPTER WAS DELETED FROM THE CORE MATERIAL, BUT I'VE INCLUDED IT FOR THE CURIOUS, OR FOR ANYONE SKEPTICAL ABOUT CLARIFYING THEIR PURPOSE BEYOND THEIR INTUITIVE UNDERSTANDING OF IT]

[I]f you know your enemies and know yourself, you will not be imperiled in a hundred battles.[210]

A. Breadth of Solution Range

Understanding the elements from which the enemy's strategy has grown—his motive, intent and desired end state—offers a broader array of offensive options against his strategy. We do not need to restrict ourselves to setting up a specific event when all we need to achieve is the *criteria*—criteria that might be present in any number of situations. We do not fight a he-said—she-said argument about what happened in the bedroom when we can pre-empt that argument by discussing how Defendant first entered the house. And similarly, a defense counsel need not limit his focus to the trial when he might achieve his client's purpose through a pre-trial settlement, motions hearing, or an appeal.[211]

---

[210] SUN TZU, ART OF WAR

[211] Some end states are preferable (the defendant paying lower damages or serving less confinement—see the discussion of utility and payoffs), but this value is still measured against the purpose.

Focusing on a single end state is a self-imposed restriction that can prevent you from seeing your best opportunities at the outset, and from changing course when a better alternative presents itself or when the situation requires a less-preferred alternative.[212]

Viewing the landscape from a perspective of purposes rather than attacking obstacles also allows you to understand what is driving other parties' actions. This can reveal potential allies in achieving certain elements of your purpose, the extent to which they will cooperate, the point at which resistance becomes likely, and whether that resistance will be active and determined, or passive or short-lived.[213]

Motives can also help gain the compliance of other parties and possibly

---

[212] You might achieve your purpose, for example, through changing perceptions rather than changing anything tangible. E.g. Having supermodels serving champagne on bullet train would be cheaper and increase satisfaction more than widening the rails to provide a smoother ride.
http://www.ted.com/talks/rory_sutherland_life_lessons_from_an_ad_man.html.

Or, consider the Hellenistic Delian League, wherein Athens abandoned the policy of making subject states pay tribute in favor of placing an ad velorum tax on merchants (a cost they passed on to consumers). A dispersed tax paid by merchants was merely an annoyance to merchants (and to the smaller pool of educated consumers), while paying tribute had been an affront to national dignity.

Moving away from perception to (mostly) tangible action, consider the environmental protection activities of The Nature Conservancy. To protect environmentally significant land, the organization would raise funds and then purchase it. However, as the organization assessed possible operations in California they realized the state held far more critical acreage than they could ever hope to purchase. By focusing on their purpose rather than their usual desired end state, they envisioned and pursued multiple overlapping solutions: promoting protective legislation (which enabled them to protect ocean areas, which had not been possible through their prior land purchases), engaged in information operations (e.g. framing "that big plot of scrub brush off the interstate" into "The Mount Hamilton Wilderness Area"), and purchasing inexpensive conservation easements on some tracts. Seeing the purpose beyond the obstacles and beyond their original desired end state presented them with new opportunities. See, CHIP HEATH & DAN HEATH, MADE TO STICK: WHY SOME IDEAS SURVIVE AND OTHERS DIE, Kindle Edition, location 1619.

[213] See gen DIXIT & NALEBUFF supra note 23.

even inspire them. People do not spring to action because a plan is clever or well-drafted. People are motivated by common beliefs and by inspirational leaders, they enlist in causes.

B. Efficient Use of Resources

Do nothing which is of no use.[214]

During litigation, and especially in trial, you near task saturation. Your limited time and other resources become a source of friction, preventing you from completing everything you need to accomplish. You must conserve resources.[215] Fighting over irrelevant issues wastes time and effort,[216] and can cost credibility. Remaining focused on your purpose allows you to quickly identify and prioritize what must be done, allowing you forego the unnecessary and to indulge in convenient tasks only when you have resources available.[217] It tells you what you must defend, and where you can efficiently spend your credibility and political capital.

C. Staying on Course

---

[214] MUSASHI MIYAMOTO, GO RIN NO SHO (1645)

[215] See the discussion of time in the OODA Loop section, below.

[216] In World War I, Germany used the manpower freed by Russia's withdrawal from the war to shift power west and break through the Allied lines in the Michael Offensive. Their original purpose was pushing the British into the channel and capturing the channel ports. However after breaking through the allied lines and two successful days of combat, the German high command decided to ignore their original purpose and ordered the German forces to disregard the channel ports and continue west. The Germans outstripped their supply lines and as malnourished troops fell to eating and drinking at each town and supply depot they captured, momentum was lost and the offensive stalled. Eventually the Germans selected the Allied rail hub at Amiens as a new objective, but by this time the allied forces were prepared to stop them. Thus, the German high command wasted the additional resources gained by Russia's withdrawal and the original momentum of their offensive by failing to focus on their purpose.

[217] This is not to say an attorney should (figuratively) tuck his chin and run full-steam at the objective. Deception, feints, and indirect routes are not wasted if they pass a cost-benefit analysis, increasing the chance of success enough to justify the expenditure of resources.

In courtrooms there are advocates who become entangled in irrelevant issues by opposing counsel or sabotage their own cases by attacking the wrong obstacle. They lose because while chasing this or that mirage, they failed to accomplish what they needed to.

By not being clear in your purpose, you may preclude some part of what you had hoped to accomplish. This happens even when you are unopposed, but staying on course becomes even harder when opposing counsel and witnesses are trying to shift the situation along other channels, and when anger, pride, arrogance or greed steer you toward certain courses of action, pulling you toward strategic drift. But a clear purpose serves as a beacon on the foggy, dancing landscape, and as a heuristic, allowing you to identify what you need to address, letting you see with greater speed and clarity where you can and cannot give ground and still accomplish your purpose.

D. De-Conflicting Purposes

When we proceed with multiple purposes that are only vaguely defined we may not realize there is a conflict between them until it creates a problem (and problems, of course, increase our level of friction). Even if we believe we are pursuing a singular purpose, it may reveal itself to be multiple goals, and these may preempt each other wholly or in part, or the conflict may be between our immediate purpose and our personal values or ethos.[218]   In reality, such conflicts can span a variety of beliefs and motives.

An attorney desires to grow his business and has many potential clients whose business he has to turn down due to lack of staff. However his efforts to hire additional support staff were continually thwarted by high employee turn-over in his company stemming from his need to dominate and bully his subordinates. The entrepreneur's desired end-state of a larger business is thwarted by a conflicting motive to dominate and bully.

---

[218] You have likely seen many dramas where the protagonist has to choose between career advancement and integrity or family. For example, Israel has a powerful motive to reduce terrorism, but they also desire to punish terrorists. At first glance these goals appear compatible, but when reprisals surpass "an eye for an eye" they can actually generate more terrorists than are killed. Without clarifying goals we can pursue counterproductive methods. *See* JOHN M. COLLINS, MILITARY STRATEGY: PRINCIPLES, PRACTICES, AND HISTORICAL PERSPECTIVES 65-66

Depending on the nature of a conflict in motives, or beliefs, people will naturally desire to rectify them.[219] However when rectifying them is not easily done, bounded rationality offers the option of justifying or deny the inherently illogical, as when anti-abortion (pro-life) activists kill doctors, denying that life is sacred to preserve life because it is sacred, or shift blame. When a party has not yet confronted the conflict, it may be leveraged against him to increase his level of friction. You will benefit by clarifying your and your client's purposes in your own mind during preparation rather than letting them linger into the trial phase when the landscape begins to dance more erratically and the level of friction begins to rise.

E. Backward Planning

Aristotle notes that once the final cause (the purpose) is in place, the other causes follow by necessity.[220] We will see clearly what he meant in the discussion on developing Lines of Operations (LOOs), below. Starting with a clearly defined purpose facilitates rapid backward planning where, given our purpose, we can quickly identify the end state with the greatest potential, and from the end state we see which factors our plan must account for, and from there, the succession of actions we must take. In this way, the time invested in clarifying purpose yields time and effort savings, and provides higher levels of confidence and clarity of direction during course of action development.

---

[219] This is "cognitive dissonance."

[220] *See* ARISTOTLE *supra* note 148.

APPENDIX C ➤ ANTICIPATING AN ADVERSARY COMPLETING THE ACT PHASE

[THIS SECTION WAS EXCISED FROM THE CORE TEXT AS UNNECESSARY. DESPITE IT NOT BEING FULLY DEVELOPED, I'VE INCLUDED IT AS AN APPENDIX FOR THE CURIOUS]

A. Mitigating

The act phase can also be attacked by mitigating, reducing or neutralizing the effects of his actions. If the opponent can foresee the potential mitigation, it is a form of deterrent. If not, then while not affecting his OODA Loop, it remains a means of addressing his action. And to the extent this increases his level of friction, it will contribute to a maneuver strategy. [221]

The methods of dampening the effects of individual COAs are entirely tactical (e.g. discrediting witnesses or deconstructing argument). Strategically, the effects of most or all of his possible COAs can be dampened by destroying opposing counsels credibility or preventing him from communicating effectively or building rapport with the jurors.[222]

---

[221] Boyd states: "Morally-mentally-physically isolate our adversaries from their allies and outside support as well as isolate them from one another, in order to: magnify their internal friction, produce paralysis, bring about their collapse; and/or bring about a change in their political/economic/social philosophy so that they can no longer inhibit our vitality and growth."

[222] This is a matter of strategy, as it generally requires a succession of tactics impacting various areas to destroy a counsel's credibility or to so fluster a counsel that he cannot communicate.

B. Counterstrike

Counterstrikes await and agent's offense to use it against him.   A counterstrike is not a counterattack or riposte. A riposte absorbs the blow of the attack, then responds (hopefully capitalizing on the adversary's disorganization following a failed offense), while a counterstrike uses the attack as a foci or a means of harming the other party. For example, with a counterattack when they say, "This happened," you counterattack with, "No, that happened." With a counterstrike, on the other hand, you would respond with, "Yes, but…" You use their offense against them, either incorporating it into your argument or discrediting their entire position.

Defense counsel, for example, often base their case on pulling apart what the prosecutor or plaintiff's attorney has put forward, and prosecutors and plaintiffs who can meet the elements of their case with somewhat bare circumstantial evidence, bait the defense to produce some sort of alibi or explanation then assert to the jury that defendant must be guilty/liable because his explanation or alibi has holes in it.

However, counterstrike offers still greater possibilities. A very mild example of the former type of counterstrike appeared in the opening case study when after the defense offered that no one else had broken into Mrs. V's house, the government took that assertion to bolster their argument that Defendant must have exploited his opportunity to unlock the back door ahead of time.

Another example occurred in a theft prosecution where the defendant's mother, a very likeable woman, testified that one of the allegedly stolen items found on defendant (a non-serialize, fungible item) could not be the stolen item in question because she had seen a person give such an item to defendant prior to the alleged theft. The prosecutor did not counterattack. Instead he drew out her description of the gifted item, then later in closing argument brushed aside her testimony saying he did not dispute her, but that based on differences between what she saw and the item in question, she was describing an item other than the stolen one found on the defendant. In this way, he used counterstrike to avoid a verbal dispute with a likeable witness, or even needing to disprove what she claimed she saw.[223]

---

[223] Note also that the prosecutor's response reflected proper orientation. He did not view the testimony as this person is an obstacle and must be attacked. Instead he saw a way that the person became irrelevant to achieving his purpose of proving that the defendant had stolen this (among other) items.

(This also allowed the jury to avoid the psychological discomfort of implying the likeable woman was a liar by convicting her son).

Counterstrike demands flexibility on your part. You must cede the initiative and allow the opponent to act as he desires, and you must be prepared for his action to be something other than what you predicted. It also requires the tactical skill of getting the opponent to commit to his offense so that he does not back away from it as your counterstrike unfolds.

C. Fabian Strategy

The Fabian strategy is a defensive approach named for Quintus Fabius, a Roman general who sought to deal with Hannibal's invasion of the Italic peninsula by simply avoiding decisive conflict and letting him exhaust himself in the foreign land. Unfortunately, (and this is an object lesson to attorneys, who must answer to clients) while the Roman senate disliked having their legions slaughtered by Hannibal under the commanders who preceded Fabius, they lacked the political will to let Hannibal exhaust himself at their expense. As a result Fabius was dismissed and his strategy not carried to fruition.[224]

In current parlance, a Fabian strategy is a defense based upon avoiding decisive engagement while, perhaps gradually, indecisively attriting the opponent, and letting him wear himself out striking blows that land nowhere. It includes, but does not require, "scorched earth" responses, where anything the opponent might use is destroyed before he gets to it.

The Fabian strategy is generally countered by threatening the enemy in a critical spot that will force decisive battle.

---

[224] Instead, the Romans attacked Carthage (the leading city on behalf of which Hannibal fought) resulting in Hannibal's recall from Italy to defend the city.

APPENDIX D ➤ THE DANCING LANDSCAPE

[THIS SECTION WAS EXCISED FROM THE CORE TEXT AS IT PROVIDES MORE INFORMATION THAN IS NECESSARY TO UNDERSTAND THE FUNDAMENTAL CONCEPT HEREIN. DESPITE IT NOT BEING FULLY DEVELOPED, I'VE INCLUDED IT AS AN APPENDIX FOR THOSE SEEKING TO EXPAND THEIR UNDERSTANDING]

Nothing is permanent except change.[225]

[A] dancing landscape… has a constantly changing topography. This occurs because the factors that describe the landscape are constantly fluctuating.[226]

A host of variables affect the outcome of any trial. People shape some of these variables, such as clarity of presentation, question order, witness order, admissibility, etc. Events beyond any single person's control affect others, for example weather, laryngitis, or power failures. All these variables interconnect to form a map of our situation, the terrain of our competitive landscape. We can best understand this terrain by first examining a single feature in isolation, then drawing back for a broader view.

---

[225] J.B.M. VRANKEN, EXPLORING THE JURIST'S FRAME OF MIND 64 (2006)(quoting Heraclitus); Ghandi's take on the matter is that "Only Truth is permanent," which is interesting in the context of the discussion of fog, above. Without contradicting Ghandi, we may observe that while lies may not be permanent, they can be highly persistent.

[226] Gastle & Boughs *supra* note 68.

1. A Single Terrain Feature

The number of questions you will ask Witness A on direct examination is one of the variables that will affect the terrain feature of "Witness A's" effectiveness. Assume, just for this hypothetical, that all of the other variables related to A's effectiveness remain fixed and the only thing that can change Witness A's effectiveness is the number of questions we ask him on direct examination.

If we ask him too few questions, the jury will not understand the points we need them to grasp, if we ask too many, our message will be lost in the mass of irrelevance, or evaporate in the jurors' stupor of boredom. Somewhere between too few and too many lies an optimal number of questions.

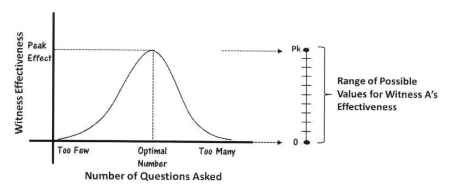

Witness A's effect on the trial might fall at any point along the curve, so depending on how many questions we ask, A's effectiveness can be anywhere between 0 and the peak value (as seen at the right of the figure). If we isolate any single variable among the dozens that affect Witness A's credibility, a similar graph could be drawn for each.

2. More Variables

Of course, the variables are not isolated. They are highly interconnected. A number of variables in combination will push Witness

A's effectiveness up or down.[227] For instance, the witnesses he follows or precedes might enhance or reduce his credibility. Opposing counsel might expose a bias. Witness A might be over- or under-caffeinated and become more engaging, or ramble unintelligibly. Each variation of presentation (witness order, bias, amount of caffeine, and dozens of others) will affect his overall effectiveness. These variables form a network.

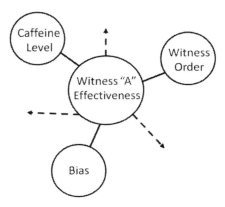

Each different mix of variables will set up a different possible bell curve for "Witness A Effectiveness." Our network graphic fails to capture this. Of course, putting all these possible combinations of variables on a graph is not an easily done, either.

---

[227] LEWIN, *supra* note 70 at 240 ("To understand or to predict behavior, the person and his environment have to be considered as one constellation of interdependent factors").

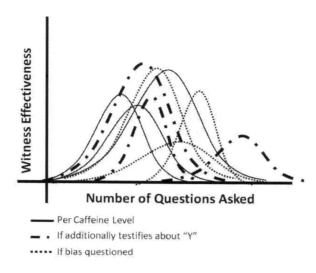

——— Per Caffeine Level

— ▪ If additionally testifies about "Y"

▪▪▪▪▪ If bias questioned

Another shortcoming of our original network diagram is that it fails to capture the magnitude of the complete network. As strategists we cannot consider Witness A's testimony in isolation. It is not an end unto itself. The overall perception of the jury as they enter deliberations is more important than Witness A's effectiveness or any other single variable. So, the network we are concerned with is far more expansive.

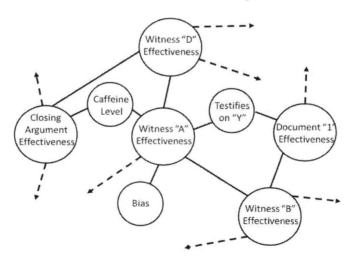

If we attempt to install the height aspect of the original bell curves to our network, we would be looking at our strategic landscape in three dimensions.

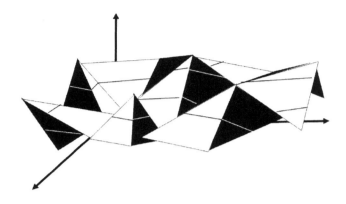

As you can see, the strategic terrain for our trial is extremely rugged. And more than just rugged, it is about to move.

3. Movement

If we unleash our independent agents upon the terrain of interconnected variables, they will push variables up and down.[228] Sometimes this will be the result of direct action, as when the judge denigrates or praises a witness, or documentary evidence contradicts testimony. But there are also second order effects from ripples, where variables converge and build momentum off each other's effects (called unanticipated influences[229]), and unintended consequences.[230]

---

[228] *Id.*at 240 ("To understand or to predict behavior, the person and his environment have to be considered as one constellation of interdependent factors").

[229] For example, if two eyewitnesses differ on minor details, and you establish that they both have flawless recollection, the effects will converge with an emergent property: one or both of the eyewitnesses will appear to be fabricating testimony.

[230] *See, e.g.,* JOHN MANSFIELD, THE NATURE OF CHANGE OR THE LAW OF UNINTENDED CONSEQUENCES (2010).

There are also perverse incentives, as when the judge's instruction to disregard a piece of evidence gives it new importance in the juror's eyes.[231] Not all variables interconnect and depend upon others but, for those that do, changing the value of one will shift the others. From the moment an attorney receives a case until he finally clears it, the strategic terrain will be undulating, dancing, as he acts and others respond, as he attempts to counter the moves of others, and as random events occur.

---

[231] Commonly called the "Streisand Effect." *See, e.g.,* EVGENY MOROZOV, *Living with the Streisand Effect,* N.Y. TIMES Dec. 26, 2008, (accessed Dec. 3, 2011, 5:36 PM) http://www.nytimes.com/2008/12/26/opinion/26iht-edmorozov.1.18937733.html.

ABOUT THE AUTHOR

Andrew Dreier is a Lieutenant Colonel in the Army JAG Corps who also speaks and consults on strategy and produces the blog *5 Minutes on Strategy* [5minstrat.blogspot.com]

LtCol Dreier served in naval intelligence during the last years of the Cold War, took part in Operation Classic Resolve (the suppression of an attempted coup d' etat in the Philippines) and in Operation Ernest Will (protecting shipping in the Persian Gulf during the Iran-Iraq War). He deployed aboard USS Midway under Navy Captain (later Vice Admiral) A.K. Cebrowski, a pioneer in network-centric warfare.

As a Marine Corps Judge Advocate, Lt Col Dreier tried nearly three hundred courts martial. He also took part in the U.S. invasion of Iraq in 2003, and assisted in planning and carrying out the reconstruction effort in Wasit Province under Task Force Tarawa and 3rd Battalion, 23rd Marines. He served as Plans officer for the Marine Corps Embassy Security Group (State Department), Deputy Staff Judge Advocate for Marine Corps Special Operations Command, as a Strategic Policy Planner for U.S. Forces Afghanistan (under General David Petraeus), and as Chief of Prioritization (a function analogous to targeting) and Lead Prioritization Planner for the anti-corruption Combined, Joint Task Force-Shafafiyat under then-Brigadier General H.R. McMaster.

He holds an LL.M. in Military Law from the U.S. Army JAG School, a J.D. from the Boston University School of Law, a B.A. in History from Worcester State College, and graduated from the Marine Corps' Amphibious Warfare School—two decades after John Boyd introduced his OODA Loop concept there.

Made in United States
Orlando, FL
15 March 2022

15842961R00065